Walter Lecky

Mr. Billy Buttons

A Novel

Walter Lecky

Mr. Billy Buttons
A Novel

ISBN/EAN: 9783742831811

Manufactured in Europe, USA, Canada, Australia, Japa

Cover: Foto ©Andreas Hilbeck / pixelio.de

Manufactured and distributed by brebook publishing software (www.brebook.com)

Walter Lecky

Mr. Billy Buttons

MR. BILLY BUTTONS.

A NOVEL.

BY

WALTER LECKY.

SECOND EDITION.

NEW YORK, CINCINNATI, CHICAGO:
BENZIGER BROTHERS,
Printers to the Holy Apostolic See.
1896.

Dedication.

THIS STORY OF MR. BILLY BUTTONS IS DEDICATED TO
THE ONE WHO FIRST VIEWED IT WITH FAVOR—
TO MY FRIEND

RICHARD MALCOLM JOHNSTON,

AUTHOR OF

THE "DUKESBOROUGH TALES,"

ETC.

CONTENTS.

CHAPTER		PAGE
I.	SKINNY BENOIT,	1
II.	BILLY BUTTONS RELATES,	34
III.	BUTTONS' LOST LOVE,	54
IV.	THE COMING OF SLITHERS,	74
V.	THE WOOING OF MILLY,	90
VI.	SKINNY BENOIT'S SON,	121
VII.	THE RETURN OF CORKEY SLITHERS,	139
VIII.	AN OLD MUSICIAN,	157
IX.	PÈRE MONNIER,	184
X.	HOME AT LAST,	208
XI.	THE PASSING OF BILLY BUTTONS,	240

MR. BILLY BUTTONS.

CHAPTER I.

SKINNY BENOIT.

"A COUNTRY doctor leads a strange life; that is a saying of one of them. His life is one of sacrifice." Those words I wrote in my diary long ago, before these wild hills became my friends. It is an opinion of mine that to enjoy Nature you must be on speaking terms with her. Toby, my good gray nag, seems to know this. No sooner does he come to a lovely snatch of scenery than his usual quick jog becomes a sedate walk. A friend of mine called Toby a brute; it was strange on my part to resent it—why I could not explain. Perhaps I was thinking of Toby being able to feast his eyes on nature, while so many men, so far removed from the brute,—I follow the moralists,—would find in these same scenes nothing to give delight. When I was a younger man I had written, as I have said, that a doctor's life was one of sacrifice; now that I have passed the fifties I see no reason to change that entry in my diary. My life has been a hard one, full of peril. Our little village lies in these mountains isolated from railways—"which means," said a New-Yorker, Dr. Jenks, "from civilization." The nearest town lies twenty miles to the south, and that by a narrow mountain road. In winter this road is snow-bound, and Snipeville— for that is the name of our village—settles down to cut logs: some logs, such as spruce and balsam, for Dixon's pulp-mill; others for Parker's saw-mill. The village store has been well supplied in the autumn with teas, sugars, coffees, and canned fruits, so there is no want of what we call here the luxuries of life. Every family has killed its fat hog and salted him, filled the cellar with potatoes, cabbages, turnips, carrots, a few beets, and stacked the yard with piles of fuel. We are poor, it is true, but our poverty is of a different sort from that felt by the toilers in the city. Jamsey Duquette sold his farm three years ago and went East. He was glad to come back to the mountains. "Doctor," says he, "when you have to buy everything, even the water, and live in three rooms not as big as a hencoop, and never see a hill, or bit of grass, or anything that you were brought up to, you get your senses back and long to see Snipeville." I had this thought of Jamsey's in my mind when Toby passed Slippery Creek, as he rounded Owl's Head. As was his wont, he became sedate. I lay back in my sleigh, cosey in my furs, chatting with the snow-crowned hills and the frozen Salmon River. Now and then that inner Me, one of the most loving of companions, suggested that if my life was hard the pleasure of such scenes as lay before me, and the robust health to enjoy them, more than repaid the sacrifice.

From behind a few straggling choke-cherry bushes came a wild, plaintive laugh. Toby stopped. William Buttons, of Squidville, avows that my horse knows when some one needs my service. It is the old story: if a man or brute shows some signs of intelligence more than the ordinary our imagination supplies the supernatural.

"Who's there?" and I peered into the cherries. "It's me, doctor," she answered; and crazed Jenny Sauvé jumped from her hiding-place, patted Toby's head, gave him a few dried brown leaves to eat, and then seated herself beside me.

"Jenny's a good girl to-day?" Jenny shook her head.

"Where was Jenny going?"

Another wild, plaintive laugh. "Jenny was a pretty girl." The handsome face, with the strange, fiery, wandering blue eyes, curved in suppressed laughter. It has always been a strange thing to me the pleasure that idiots take in being praised. This reminds me that more than twenty years ago I prepared a paper on the "Sensibility of Idiots to Flattery." I read it to Jenks; he laughed at it, called it unscientific. Jenks is a New York specialist, which means unbounded egotism, linked with scepticism of other men's works.

"Will I drive Jenny to the store?"

"No, no, doctor; go to Skinny Benoit's. Skinny is sick."

"Very bad, Jenny?"

"She cry much; one tooth," and, laughing, Jenny, opening her mouth, beat time on her pearly teeth with the long nail of her index finger. Here I admit that I am no specialist, to use a phrase of Blind Cagy's. I am an all-round man. Tooth-pulling is one of my arts, and it was easy to see, by Jenny, that my service as a dentist was required at Skinny Benoit's. I gave Jenny a few pennies and told her to sing me a song. She clutched the coins in her right hand, hiding them in the folds of her bare-worn calico gown, while she used the left hand to brush back the long, unkempt, vagrant yellow curls, tossed to and fro by the sharp, snappy breeze. A quick shake of the head, like a high-bred horse setting out to win, and she sang in a jerky, sad way:

> "J'ai vu la fille du meunier:
>   Comme est belle!
>   Avec son bonnet de dentelle
>   Qui voltige au vent printanier.
>   J'ai vu la fille du meunier,
>   La belle fille,
>   Au gai,
>   Au gai,
>   Chantait le long de la charmille."

I turned Toby's head and took the narrow wood road that leads to Skinny's.

Henriette Benoit—better known as Skinny, on account of her emaciated form—lived in a little maple grove that yielded enough syrup to smear her morning buckwheat cakes. The house was a log one, the usual kind to be met with in these mountains. Before the door lay a few half-rotten logs, with an axe carelessly stuck in the butt-end of one of them. I drove to the rickety door, that had been years ago smeared with common red paint, and jumped from the sleigh. Jenny, with the grace and ease of a fawn, had preceded me, and while I tied Toby to the half-rotten logs she threw affectionately over his shoulders my big buffalo-robe, and went in search of dry leaves, the only dish the poor thing was able to procure for him. I pulled the latch-string and entered Skinny's house. There is no ceremony, no "bowing and scraping," to use a phrase of William Buttons, about a country doctor. The women folks are always glad to see him, either on account of present or impending ills.

Skinny sat near the stove, with a huge towel tightly drawn around her head. As she rocked herself on her rickety chair she muttered, "Ah me! ah mi! ah mo!" ending in a long-drawn sigh. This reminded me that I had written in the medical paper, tabooed by Jenks as unscientific, "that a great deal of sorrow escapes by way of music."

"What's the matter, Mrs. Benoit?" I asked, and put my medical chest on the plain deal table, littered with dishes and broken crockery that Jenny had got from the neighbors.

"Take a seat, doctor, and warm yourself; it's blustering out," and Skinny rose from the only chair she possessed, and sat on a low stool. The chair, stool, and rough deal table were the only furniture that she owned. For a bed she had placed some oat straw in one corner of the cabin. On this was thrown a worn mattress of dried shavings, a few old quilts, whose faded colors told of long-gone splendor, and a threadbare spread. Despite the scanty furnishings of her home, there was about it an air of neatness and cleanliness.

On the walls were hung a few religious pictures, gotten from a Jewish pedlar in exchange for maple-syrup, and a large framed picture of a country store in Canada, with a young man and woman standing in the door full of smiles and happiness. It required some effort to believe that that fair young bride was no other than the towelled Skinny. "Fact is a harder pill to swallow than fiction," is the truest thing that Buttons spat out.

"You're a great one, Granny Benoit, to make such a fuss about a stump."

I opened my chest. Skinny took no notice

of my banter, but slowly unfolded the towel from her head; this done, she pityingly glanced at me with her little bloodshot eyes, and in evident pain opened her mouth. I held the forceps in my right hand, behind my back, while I curved my left, making a rest of it for her old white head.

"Take the chair; sit higher, and lean back your head in my arm, granny."

"Anything you say, doctor," said Skinny, following my commands. A look into the mouth was sufficient to reveal the cause of her pain. The one tooth—the only reminder left of the pearly row so prominent in the framed picture—had got to go. To use one of our mountain phrases, "For years it had stood there alone, like a burnt pine log in a bit of cleared land."

"Are you ready, granny?"

"No, doctor, not yet; let me see him before you pull him — he's the last," and a tear wriggled down, winding its way through the brown, drooping wrinkles of her face.

Skinny rose from the chair, pulled out the table-drawer, and brought out a broken looking-glass. She opened her mouth and gazed long and wistfully at the solitary stump, the cause of all her woe. I leaned against the rickety chair, and this thought, which I intend to put in my diary as soon as I go home, came: "Man's a queer animal wedded to his infirmities."

"I'm ready now, doctor," and Skinny was in her old position. "The poor fellow has got to go," said granny, "and the sooner the better. I won't flinch an inch, doctor; but for Heaven's sake don't break it, do your job thorough."

I nodded assent—a quick jerk and the decayed stump, the last bit of her beauty, as Skinny called it, lay in the palm of her hand. A sad smile hovered over her face as the gaunt fingers lovingly rolled it in a gingham rag and put it away in a little wallet that she carried in her bosom.

"Faith, granny," said I as I wiped my fingers with a piece of batting, "you think more of your enemies than I would. You take them to your heart." Skinny made a feint to smile. Looking up at the framed picture, "I once was proud of these same teeth," said she, "and of this old face. God forgive my vanity! That was long ago, in the days of the framed picture. I was not a bad-looking girl either, if I do say it, ugly as I am now. But what's the use of filling strangers ears with the things that made Skinny as she is?" She buried her head in her towel and was silent.

It seems to me that gossip is half the life of a country physician. I know it is the fashion of writers to hurl hard names against gossip; but take it out of life, and surely then life is not worth living. The philosophers have been great gossipers: that, by the way, is worthy of my diary. I like to gossip. Open confessions, says the moralist, are good for the soul. My curiosity was excited, my appetite whetted, by granny's words and way. It was not for nothing that she burrowed in the towel. I had extracted granny's tooth: could I not extract through gossip the story of her early life, and know something of the framed picture?

The neighbors had declared that granny came to the log cabin years ago, when the crazy girl was but a baby; from where she was never known to tell. I pulled the stool nearer the stove, and sat down by Skinny's side.

"Will I get cold without that towel?" said Skinny.

"No, granny; the old stump drawn, all will be well."

"Ay, the old stump," muttered Skinny as

she told me, unasked, the story of the framed picture—the story of a life.

It may be a weakness of mine to listen to my neighbors' business, but it is one that has given me much pleasure. Women are as supple as ivy plants, is a mountain saying. They want to lean on something. There is no oak like a sympathetic listener. Skinny's tale was full of interest to me, and I take it for granted that there are a large class in this world with the same kind of feeling as a country doctor. To them I will owe no apology for telling the tale, and that in Skinny's homely way.

"My father came from Lyons," said she, resting her head on the shut knuckles of the left hand, "and settled in Montreal. He had not been long in that city when he fell in love, and married the Widow Le May, that kept the baker-shop in Notre Dame Street. Madame Le May's first-born was me," and Skinny laughed a little broken, sorrow-fringed laugh. "She was the woman for you, doctor; she could bake more bread than half a dozen men. You don't believe it; *mais c'est vrai*. A few weeks after my birth she died." Her voice was tremulous, and tears ran down her crumpled face. "I often shut my eyes and think I see the kind of a woman my mother was. She had long black hair,—that I am sure,—and her eyes, they were as bright as coals, but black, black. Her mouth was small, and her cheeks as round and 'fat as a plum.' I described her one day to my father. '*Mon Dieu*, Henriette! it's your mother. She must be hovering round you like a butterfly; she did like you uncommon well.' After poor mother's death my father, who was a dancing-master, and could make nothing out of the baking, sold the shop, and opened a little school of dancing on St. Catherine Street. Here I remained until my sixteenth year, when the life-struggle became too great for my father. One day, it seems like yesterday, I was standing over the tub washing some shirts for him (he was always particular about his linen), when a young man opened the door and handed me a letter. I laid it on the dresser-shelf, thinking it meant a new pupil.

"As soon as father entered I gave him the letter. He slowly read it, spelling out the words, and hung down his head.

"'Are you sick, father?' I asked.

"'Not sick, but tired, Henriette.'

"I thought I saw a tear run down his cheeks.

"'You are crying, father,' and I dropped on his knee, put my arm about his neck, and we both cried.

"'Henriette,' said my father, drying his tears, 'you are a foolish child; you must not cry: we may be happy yet.'

"'You are not happy now, father—I know you're not,' and I pressed his old gray head to my bosom.

"'No, not happy,' he said,—his voice was like his own old fiddle when a couple of strings were broken,—'and you may as well know the cause. My little school has been shut for the last year. I could find no pupils; the sacred art of dancing is dead in Montreal. A fellow called Fournier teaches what he calls a complete course in six lessons. No one wants to study and know a thing thorough in these times, so all my pupils have gone to Fournier. Whenever I seek a pupil madame says: "M. Bourbonnais, you are too old and stiff to teach ma'm'selle."

"'*Mon Dieu*, Henriette, it maddens me—Bourbonnais, that taught in the châteaux of the Faubourg St. Germain; Bourbonnais, that danced before the empress and was complimented by Taglioni.' He jumped from his seat, and, crumpling the letter in a solid piece, threw it into the fire, and stood there watching it burn.

"'What have you been doing, father?' I said; and I pulled down his head and kissed him.

"'Doing, Henriette? Earning a poor living for all that is left to me in this world—that's you, dear. A poor living indeed, but working hard for it. Every morning before you were awake I took my fiddle, kissed you, dropped a tear on your pretty face, and went out fasting to earn our poor breakfast.

"'I went into the back streets, where I was unknown, and danced and played for a sou.

"'Some, the poorest, were glad to see Henri Bourbonnais. If they could not give him money they gave food, which I carried home in the pillow-slip that I sewed one night, while you were asleep, in the inside of my old threadbare coat. The rich passed me by in scorn. Not a few gibed me, and made fun of my music, and laughed at my dance. Ah, Henriette, it is so easy to make fun of the unfortunate! Every noon I came home smiling, lest you might guess the truth, but sad of heart. On my way I visited a little church, attracted by its flickering little altar-lamp. The lamp seemed always to be going out, yet managed to live on;

it was so like your old father for the last twelve months. In that little church, to the right-hand side of its main altar, you can see in yellow letters: "Come to Me, all ye that labor and are heavy laden, and I will refresh you." I have knelt for hours before those yellow letters, saying, I am heavy laden; and asking God to keep His promise. Will He do so? My poor old shoulders ache. Fiddling and dancing will soon be beyond me, and then, Henriette—'

"His voice broke in pieces; a big clump of sorrow choked him. I turned away my head; I could not speak.

"'Give me my fiddle, child; if we speak your old father will act silly about these things, and you will ruin your pretty face with tears. Let the fiddle do the talking.'

"The tune he played was one my mother taught him; it is pretty common in Canada with the Scotch. The best I can remember, they call it 'Highland Mary.' Big Donald McKinnon said it was written by one of his father's chums. He must have been smarter than Donald, or his father either, to have picked out of his head such a sweet song. My father liked the tune on account of mother. He used to say he had lost everything belonging to her but that bit of a tune. When he finished I took his fiddle and put it in the old green baize bag—my first piece of needle-work. I have that fiddle yet, doctor, and I would starve rather than part with it.

"He leaned his head on the chair-back and drew a long, broken, heavy sigh. Tears ran down my cheeks as I gazed on his pinched and worn old face. The old clock that he called *Willy-Wag-tail* was the only thing I could hear in the house, and its tick was as loud as the stroke of a hammer. I became afraid and ran to my father. I tried to kiss him, but his face was freezing cold. I spoke to him. I watched his mouth for an answer. Everything was so quiet except the clock. 'God!' I cried, 'You keep Your promises—my father is dead!'

"I must then have fallen to the floor. The first thing I remember was a feeling of strange pains, like the jags of a thousand needles plastered over my body. I tried to raise myself; I could not. Then, with all my strength, I tried to turn on my side, thinking to shake off the pains. Strength, did I say? I had none; and so I lay like a log. Now and then I could hear a voice, a sweet voice, telling me to open my eyes, and I could feel a soft hand pressing my cheek. The hand moved to my burning eyes, and I felt something soft, cooling, strengthening falling into them, something loosening the eyelids, putting out the fire and bidding me see. How strange was that seeing! It was as if I had been dead for years, and suddenly awoke. I was in a large room full of little white beds, in every one of which was a woman. Some were as young as me, others younger, some middle-aged, many old. What were they doing here? For by the light that fell on my bed, through the big red-curtained window, I knew it was mid-day. I tried to speak; I could not. I wanted to say one word: 'Father.' My mouth moved, but no sound came to my ear.

"Dazed, full of fear that I was mad, I shut my eyes, and again I felt the soft pressure of that hand on my cheek. I opened my eyes. Leaning over the head of my bed was a sweet face, with a big white frame around it, like the wings of a bird. I knew by the voice it was living, and that I was not mad. 'Henriette,' it said, 'do not fear; I am only Sister Marie. You are in the Hôtel Dieu. I will take the best of care of you until you are better.' Ah, doctor! when you're sick there's no music like a kind woman's tongue. The voice of Sister

Marie was worth the full of your sleigh of pills and medicine. It gave me strength then and there to turn on my side, and it thawed my tongue. I was astonished at my own speaking, it was so strong and my tongue was so easy.

"'Where is my father?' was the first question. The sister bent down her head, and in a soft way whispered in my ear, 'At rest, child;' then, turning her head, 'Yes, my old master, Henri Bourbonnais, good old soul, lies in Mount Royal. It is a trial, Henriette, the first milestone of sorrow in your life; but accept it. It is the hand of the Lord.' My eyes filled with tears; the sister faded away like a bit of chimney smoke. I saw an old man surrounded by a noisy crowd of boys, jeering and laughing at his threadbare coat. He played a fiddle and attempted a dance to its music. A window opened, a sunburnt hand tossed him a sou; he painfully stooped and picked it out of the mud, bowed his old white head, and muttered, '*Merci, madame*,' passing to another door. I followed him from door to door, from street to street, until he entered a little chapel, and I heard him cry his burden was heavy. A white figure passed and touched his forehead. The little chapel faded from view. I opened my eyes. I heard a voice saying, 'The Lord keeps His promises.' It was that of Sister Marie.

"'To be left so young, and no friends, sister.'

"'The Lord giveth and taketh as is His will,' said she; 'happy are they who submit.'

"'Happy, Sister Marie?' and I closed my weary eyes in sleep.

"St. Henri is a little town a few miles outside of Montreal." The very name brought tears to granny's eyes. Her story was gaining in interest. I threw a big pine log on the smouldering coals, while Skinny continued:

"Doctor, you don't know how much I love that little town. As soon as I was well the sisters found me a place there with a family called Cartier. It was so lonely at first that I wanted to die and be with father. One day Dr. Cartier sent me to Napoleon La Flamme's for a loaf of bread. Napoleon kept his little shop a few doors' distant. It was a neat little place, and Napoleon, if I do say it, was such a *bon garçon*. Look at his picture, doctor, beside me. It's as like him as two peas on the one bush. My picture has changed for the worse.

"When I went into his shop he was all smiles. He left half a dozen of his customers waiting and came to me. '*Comment ça vous,*

Ma'm'selle Bourbonnais?' he said; and then I saw all the customers winking and shaking their heads. I would have cried then had not Jenny Lavoie said to Victoria Borsu, 'I don't see what Napoleon sees in that black thing.' That was me. After that I was mad, and made up my mind to spite them. 'I am very well, Mr. Napoleon La Flamme,' said I; 'and how be yourself?' 'Between fairly and middling,' said he, 'Ma'm'selle Bourbonnais;' and he wrapped my loaf in white paper,—that was the best kind he had in the store,—and tied it with a red string.

"'That will hold, I'll warrant you, Ma'm'selle Bourbonnais.' I took my loaf and went out. Victoria and Jenny made faces at me; even Mrs. Chapuis, that lives next door to Cartier's and goes to church every morning, called me Montreal *boue*. When I was on the front step I could hear Napoleon saying, 'Girls, she's a rattler.' I was so proud that I let the loaf fall on the ground. Only for the red string and the white paper the loaf would have been destroyed outright.

Dr. Cartier was a little bit of a man, always scolding about things that did not concern him. Mrs. Cartier was a big, raw-boned woman, that spent her time lying on a sofa reading novels—

that kind of books with yellow covers. I was to do all the housework, besides washing two dirty-looking dogs, Gyp and Fan, in the suds every Saturday. One Saturday I put Gyp in the tub and turned the kettle-spout on his back. I reckon it was a little warm, for he did what he had never done before—jumped from the tub yelling like a scalded young one, and ran to Mrs. Cartier, spotting all her book, as she said, with dirty water. My mistress called the doctor and told him that I had warmed Gyp up to boiling. Then, shaking her finger at me and turning to her husband, she said, 'Love, attend to that asylum girl; this book is so interesting.' The doctor ran at me like a bear, danced all around me, called me hard names, threatened me with prison, and ended by slapping my face. As soon as he left the kitchen I took my hat and went down to Napoleon's shop. There was nobody in but Napoleon. As soon as I saw him I began to cry and wish myself dead.

"'Henriette,' said Napoleon, fixing me a seat on a cracker-barrel and sitting down by my side, 'these Cartiers are a low set. They sprung from nothing, as you can easy see. They have killed a dozen girls, and they'll kill you if you don't get out. Now, I'm lonely. I have a good store, five hundred dollars in bank, two cows and a year-old heifer, all in tip-top condition. I have a home, you're out of a home; let us strike a bargain. If you're in it let me kiss you to seal it,' and he stretched his neck under my mouth.

"I do not know how it happened, but, law me, doctor, what a powerful kiss Napoleon gave me! 'My brand is on you now,' says he, 'and you need have no fear for the Cartiers.'

"Just then Jenny Lavoie came in with a terrible face on her. 'Shake,' says Napoleon; 'Henriette and I are engaged. Take a bid to the wedding.' Jenny walked up to me and kissed me, whispering in my ear that it was her that put Napoleon's mind on me as just the thing he wanted. You don't know, doctor, how much deceit and lying there is in Canada. The wedding was a grand affair. Everybody was asked and everybody came. It lasted three days, with a new fiddler every night. That first year was all joy, doctor." And Skinny, possibly comparing it with the gloomy years that followed it, used the towel on her reeking, bloodshot eyes.

"They say that every calm calls a storm;

it was so with me,' continued Skinny. "About a year after the birth of my son Frank there came what Napoleon called a crash. Money left the country all at once, and Napoleon's books were filled with trust. The best farmers had not a sou. On an evil day Napoleon received a letter from James Weeks — him that runs the Hunter's Paradise in Squidville. The prospects, wrote Jim, are on the ups, and a good thing might be made by logging it on the Salmon River. So Napoleon sold his little shop — that's the picture of it that's framed — and came to Squidville. Work was scarce that winter, so in the next fall Napoleon went to guiding."

Her voice was low, passion-tossed, and tremulous. "Jim Weeks got him a party from New York; their name was Jenks. There was in that party Dr. Jenks, his wife, and his son — a young man of twenty-three or thereabouts."

Tears were flowing freely from granny's eyes.

"The first day's hunt was started in the direction of Mud Pond, Blind Cagy putting out the dogs, as he knew the lie of the country better than Napoleon. At the burnt hill Cagy came on a doe and two fawns. The dogs tracked the fawns; and you know how fawns fool a dog, scooting here and there; so Napoleon, thinking to help the dogs a bit, crept through the brush, keeping his eye peeled, as Cagy said, for the old one, that was pretty nigh the youngsters. Young Jenks, who was watching one of the runways, saw him, and, having no learning about hunting, thought he was a deer. He took aim and fired, killing poor Napoleon on the spot.

"That's what there is to that picture, doctor."

Just then laughing Jenny came in singing:

> "Monsieur d'Marlbrook est mort,
> Mironton, mironton, mirontaine;
> Monsieur d'Marlbrook est mort,
> Est mort et entérré."

"What about Jenny?" I asked.

Skinny was wiping her eyes with the towel. Looking out on the coming darkness, in a broken way she muttered:

"The night's a bad one; the wind is up, and there may be a drift; besides, Toby has the shivers. Go home, doctor; that's another story, to be told some other day."

"Come, Jenny," said Skinny, turning to the child, "the big black dog is out; get to bed, or he'll eat you up."

The sweet voice was silent; the mirth had flown. Crouched in a corner, with wild, glittering eyes and painful face, was Jenny Sauvé.

I went out, jumped into my cutter, wrapped myself in fur, and away went Toby.

CHAPTER II.

BILLY BUTTONS RELATES.

There were but two holidays in Squidville: one was election-day, when all the choppers were supposed to show their colors and vote for Pink or Punk, as their "convictions were in it," to use one of their characteristic phrases; the other was the Fourth of July, when the surrounding towns as far as Snipeville came in a body to celebrate that glorious day in front of Jim Weeks' hotel.

Election-day was mostly passed in arguing the respective differences of the two great political parties; or listening to the slippery wisdom of Weeks, who, belonging to neither party, was considered of both. Women were not allowed "to twang their muzzle"—another Squidville saying—on such occasions. "A woman has no more right in politics than a crow in a cornfield," said Buttons to Charlie Parker, who had spent a winter in Oberlin College, and came back full of women's rights and tariff. Buttons was highly applauded for his forcible utterance; even Weeks, whose verdict was final, was heard to say that "a sprinkling of college made a man a fool," as any living body could see by the ranting of that Parker lad. Buttons was not much of a hand at ciphering out the papers, but "wherever he got his pickin's he walked straight away from that Parker on the woman business." Poor Parker died soon after of lung trouble, and not a few of our folks said that it was Weeks' way of putting it that made him go off so soon.

The Fourth of July was a different kind of holiday. Jim Weeks donated his grove, and the picnic, under the auspices of the St. Jean-Baptiste Society, was an amiable affair for charity's sake. Every kind of conveyance was taken from its hiding-place and made tidy to do service on that day. Mothers for months had saved their pennies on butter and eggs to buy white waists and red skirts for their daughters. White straw hats with black bands, showy scarfs, mostly of a bright red color, and cheap, flashy jewelry, as breast-pins, rings, and watch-chains, had materially reduced the hard-earned winter's pay of the young men. What of that? It was Squidville's way; and here I remark, with

Cagy, that to set yourself up against the ways of your neighbors "shows that your roof needs shingling." Everybody was supposed to be happy on the Fourth. The old men for that day were young, and indulged in such harmless sports as running up greased poles, catching buttered pigs, or, tied in bags, running races. Women were free to gossip, cajole, coax. Man was the victim of her wiles that day, and the money gained by her arts, when the day's enjoyment was over, was lovingly given to Père Monnier, whose kindly smile was a great reward. It was the proud boast of Weeks that there was but one religion in Squidville that day, and that was love for Père Monnier, whose strong, man-loving nature had conquered creeds and races. The Fourth was a rare day, given up to music, drollery, horse-racing, and horse-trading. It came rather strange to the folks of Squidville to have another holiday added to their scanty list. Those who have stopped over a night at the Hunter's Paradise have had their ears, I reckon, filled with how came Hiram Jones' day.

Cagy tells the story well, but I prefer Buttons' way of handling it. It was while on a professional visit to Mrs. Andrieux, last winter, that I stopped with my old friend Weeks, and heard Buttons tell the story after this fashion:

Rev. Harrison Gliggins, our pastor of well-nigh five-and-forty years' standing, rich in the promises of his Maker, had passed the portals of the beyond, joined the many on the great camping-ground. Brother Gliggins was a member of the Appomattox Lodge of the G. A. R., and one of the charter members of Brimstone Lodge of I. O. O. F. The *Porcupine Pioneer* spoke of him as "a man of metallic physique, a sweet poet whose 'Bid Me Bloom Again' will last as long as the Adirondacks." To fill the place of such a man was no easy job. The congregation that he had built up and held by the spell of his voice, after his death had become disorganized. There were many causes at work to destroy the forty-five years' work of our dead brother. One of the strongest was Jim Weeks, urged by his daughter Mary to introduce a bit of music into the church. Weeks' idea was to get a melodeon and let Mary play—be, as folks said, "a kind of an organer." A good many that had sat at the feet of Brother Gliggins for thirty years would not hear of any new patented thing like one of these melodeons squealing in church. "It would," said Sal Purdy, who had led the choir during the life of Brother Gliggins, "make a pandimion in the church;" and everybody knew what Gliggins used to say: "Show me the pandimion and I'll show you Satan." Weeks' only daughter, Mary, a girl of eighteen, had spent a few months in New York City, and while there, under the distinguished teaching of Mademoiselle Grondier, had learned to play "Nearer, my God, to Thee," "Mansions in the Sky." The proud father had purchased an organ for his daughter in Malone, and set it in the most conspicuous corner of his cosey parlor. The highest tribute he could pay a friend was an invitation to this parlor, where Mary, mindful of her accomplishments, threw back her long yellow curls, casting a glance at the open music-sheets, while she sang in her soft mountain voice her treasured and envied repertory. It was the ambition of Weeks' life to have those "same bits of melody swinging through the church, and Mary just showing them from the loft that people don't go to New York for nothing." Mary had lost her mother in infancy; her father remained unmarried for the sake of the child, who was, as he delighted to tell, "the dead spit of her mother." A kind lady, who was accustomed to board at her father's hotel every summer, took a deep interest in the pretty, motherless child. After many entreaties she persuaded Weeks to let Mary pass a few months every winter in New York City.

A few weeks of her second winter's visit had passed sight-seeing, and adding a new hymn to her slender repertory, when she received a letter from her father stating that " many of the folks were a-coming over to the hymns in church, since it had been explained to them that all the churches were a-running in the music line. Even Sal Purdy, since her last visit to Mr. Perkins, of Snipeville, who boldly told her, without putting a finger in his mouth, that music was much made of in the Scriptures, was a-coming in; so you may hold yourself in readiness," wrote the proud father, " as soon as you come home, to be our organer."

A postscript added that " as yet they were without a minister, but from the many applications they hoped soon to have a man full of the Lord in their midst." Mary kissed the letter, crumpled it in her skirt-pocket, and dreamt that night of her far-off mountain home. The attractions of the great city, so strange on her first acquaintance, were becoming fascinating —

she forgot Squidville with the coming of morning. Vacation-time sped quickly. To this girl from the heart of the Adirondacks that vacation had been a fairy dream. When the time to return came a strange, wild rebellion against her dismal country life was born in her soul.

"How happy you are, Miss Grondier," she said, not daring to look her teacher in the face, "to be able to live in this great city. I am miserable. I hate that horrid Squidville. It will be so dull. Just think that in ten minutes more my train will leave here; and who knows if I shall ever come back?"

"What a beautiful station this Grand Central is," said the astute teacher, leading her pupil to other thoughts.

"Yes, it is beautiful," and Mary Weeks' eyes were filled with tears. "That's the reason I hate to leave it. Everything is beautiful in this city. To-morrow morning at eight I will get off this train,"—Mary burst into wild laughter,—"and, goodness, Miss Grondier, our depot is about the size of that coal-box. Here, look what houses are around, and what lights. Our depot is in the woods,—nothing but woods,

woods,—and the only light at this time of night is Billy Buttons' lantern, and then the half of the time it is out."

"You will soon forget this city, child," said Miss Grondier, kissing her crying pupil.

"All aboard!" said the colored porter, and the train moved out of the great city, bearing away a girlish heart.

Miss Grondier waved a handkerchief, shed a tear with some effort, and, hurrying through the depot to the street, entered a street-car homeward bound.

The train sped quickly on, past city and sleeping hamlet, entering the great forest, sounding the death-knell across lovely lakes to the wild deer that browsed among their reeds. Mary's sleep was calm and unbroken.

"Next station Ringville!" shouted the colored gentleman. Mary jumped from her cot, and in her eagerness to see the little coal-box station once more forgot the great city. The train stopped. Mary grasped her little travelling-bag and was soon on the platform in the embrace of her father.

"Mary, Mary!" shouted the frantic father, "you must never leave me again. I'm getting old. Everything is a kind of queer around the house since you left. My hotel has been a barrack for the last two months."

"That's the truest word in your life," said Buttons, grasping Mary's hand.

"I got a kind of new coat, Mary, to give you a welcome," said Cagy, cramping the wagon that was to bear away the first girl in Squidville.

"Come, Mary, jump in the wagon; I long to see you at the Hunter's Paradise. I left La Flamme's dogs to watch the premises; so I worry," said Weeks, helping his daughter to seat herself in the wagon.

"No fear," said Cagy, taking the reins.

"It's a go!" shouted Weeks, clapping his daughter's back, and away went the wagon.

Billy Buttons sauntered slowly after. His thoughts were busied on the fitness of Mrs. Poulet to be his wife, and the means of accomplishing such an arduous undertaking. He was in a jovial mood. His pipe was sending out a steady smoke, a sure sign of the inward peace of an Adirondack guide. "I'll just step in and see her," he was saying to himself, when a voice from behind shouted:

"I say, sir, is this the nearest road to Weeks'

— James Weeks, sir? I mean Weeks of the Hunter's Paradise, sir."

The stranger was a short, stout, good-looking man, bearing on the forties. One hand clutched a worn-out satchel stuffed with papers; the other held his eyeglass, and was in constant use in the vain attempt of adjusting it to either eye.

"Keep right ahead—follow the wagon-track, sir, and you cannot miss it," said Buttons. "It's the only frame house, sir, in these parts."

The stranger quickened his gait, and was soon by the side of Buttons, who eyed him suspiciously. "It's a fine healthy morning, sir," said the stranger.

"Healthy, sir—that's the word. It would almost put life in a dead man."

"Are you of these parts?"

"Yes, sir, of these very parts. I am known to everybody as William Buttons, the guide. What may be your name, sir?—if I am not a little out of my way in asking such a question."

"My name, sir," said the stranger, tugging on his satchel, "is better known in the great metropolis than in these parts. I am, sir, an evangelist, and my name, sir, is the Rev. Hiram Marcellus Jones. People call me the Sweeping Cyclone."

The smoke ceased in Buttons' pipe. He was not astonished—an Adirondack guide rarely is. Relieving the Cyclone of his scanty baggage, he asked him if, "for the sake of the nearness, would he not just cross a few fields?" The Cyclone willingly assented, and Buttons, with his mind on Poulet, save a few odd thoughts on his companion, led the way to the Hunter's Paradise.

Sunday was a lovely day. The trees were putting on their spring bonnets, and the long-lost warblers flitted in song from tree to tree, happy in their old surroundings. Here and there a few flowers cautiously peeped, reconnoitring for their hidden fellows. Although it was early in the morning, smoke crept from many a household that at this time on ordinary Sundays were accustomed to slumber. Something was agog—and that something was, as a paper posted in Weeks' hotel said, "the coming of Hiram Jones, the fertilizer of the vineyard of the Lord. Moody's only Christian rival." Hiram M. Jones, D.D., was to fill the pulpit. Weeks' organ had been carted to the church. Mary Weeks, "with new tunes," was to preside at the organ, "rendering melodies to the Lord." All these things and many more said the paper, "in," as Cagy remarked, the "finest words that ever dirtied a sheet." Weeks to his dying day claimed that Mary had not only "pasted up that notice, but had composed it out of her own skull." It may have been so, but country jealousy would have it otherwise. The little bell of Père Monnier's church sang sweetly over the hills: "It's just ten o'clock. Come all to Mass." In answer to the bell's song came the clatter of horses' hoofs, and the merry voices of old and young in the Canadian *patois*. They had to be in time, for Père Monnier was strict as to his hours of service. Following on the heels of Père Monnier's flock came a motley throng in all kinds of wagons; the Squidville stage in the lead, containing Weeks, his daughter Mary, Sal Purdy, and the Rev. Hiram Marcellus Jones. That the Cyclone in the space of a few days had converted so persistent a hater of the melodeon to a staunch supporter was, as she herself put it, "of powers other than earthly." The strange procession halted at the meeting-house—a small brick building—and entered. The exterior was severely simple, while the interior was of the homeliest description. The pews were roughly hewn—paint was too cheery for a building that was only used once a week, and then as a soul-chastiser. There was an attempt at a pulpit—the *chef-d'œuvre* of a village genius. The attempt was fantastically crowned by a huge red cushion, the gift of Gliggins' second wife. Behind the pulpit was a sofa of faded hues, whereon the minister sat during the singing of the hymns. The service was over. In front of the door little knots of men and women gathered discussing the preacher and the music — things now inseparable. The centre of one of these groups was Weeks, bowing and smiling.

As Sal Purdy came within range of his voice he shouted, " Sal, what do you think of Jones ? "

" Think, Jim Weeks ? I ain't able to think — I am about ' curmuddled.' He's an angel, that man. And, bless my soul, Jim Weeks, I wouldn't live without music. This day is surely a taste of what he called beyond ' the impirnin blue,' " was Sal's response.

" He's a Jim dandy; make no mistake about it, Sal," said Berry.

" He talks like a book. Didn't you see how he rolled his eyes, pounded the pulpit, knocked that darned cushion down?—and the whole business as unconcernedly as I would chop a log," said the usually sedate Ike Perkins.

"Well, Jim Weeks, I give in my gun," said Bill Whistler, one of the leaders of the no-music crusade. "That sermon was a corker! It was so powerful that old Middy Slack cried; and for him to cry it takes a No. 1 preacher."

Weeks was elated. To these curious remarks he had but one reply. "Boys, Jones 's the stuff. That sermon was onions to the eyes all round. Let us, on the strength of it, give him an unanimous call. All in favor shout aye; contrary, no."

There was not a dissenting voice. And it came to pass that the Rev. Hiram Marcellus Jones became pastor of the Methodist Episcopal Church of Squidville. Being a bachelor, he preferred a room in Weeks' hotel to any log cabin in Pleasant View.

Under his loving and devoted care the disorganized congregation became organized. Stray sheep entered the fold, and his power as a preacher became, as he loved to put it, "manifest for God's glory." He had many calls from the neighboring charges, and, being of a travelling disposition, he generally accepted them.

It was noticed on these occasions that Mary Weeks was his constant companion. "Her voice," said the Cyclone to a brother divine, " is a worthy instrument used by the Lord to prepare the way for my preaching."

The first year of his pastorship ended in glory. The coming year it was announced that Brother Jones, in order to carry out more satisfactorily his work in the ministry, would wed one of the " parish folks." This announcement, strange to say, caused little commotion in the usually talkative town. When it was later authoritatively stated that the maiden's name was Mary Weeks, people shook their heads in a knowing way, saying to each other, " I told you it was bound to be." That marriage was the greatest event in the checkered career of Squidville. There came nine brother divines to wish Brother Jones " days of thankfulness in the Lord," while delegations from all the surrounding settlements entered Squidville as a mark of appreciation of the " mighty revival that had come to pass, so to say, by his hands." So great was the throng of well-wishers that came to the marriage feast that the Hunter's Paradise for the first time in its history lacked accommodation.

" By crackey ! " said Buttons, as he sat on the empty soap-box viewing the long line of strange faces that passed through the corridor that led to the hotel dining-room, "these long, thin-pointed, whiskered, shouting click will eat our friend James out of house and home."

"I am not thinking, William, of other people's crooked stomachs, this very minute; but of poor Mary. You know, William, that chickens of different ages don't go very good in the same coop," said Cagy, seating himself near his inseparable friend.

"There's a chunk of truth, Cagy, in that very saying; besides, an old plaster is a poor remedy for a young sore. But it's none of our business; so let us go home."

Cagy arose, and the two old guides, sorrowing, went down the road. The guests in the dining-room sat wondering at the heaped-up plates of half a dozen good things recklessly jostling each other. Brother Jones gave the word of command, and a hundred knives and forks made a quick attack on the plates. When about half done — that is the way we calculate in these parts — Bill Whistler moved that they should name the day "Hiram Jones', and keep it till Gabriel sounds the last roll-call." Bill was a Grand Army man, and his sentiments were felt to be in the right tune. It was passed;

and after the plates were cleared, and Brother Perkins had spoken a few words of cheer, the happy couple left for Snipeville.

If Brother Jones was energetic in the days of his bachelorhood, he was doubly so after marriage. That year he founded in Squidville an Endeavor Society, a savings-bank for the choppers, and, in partnership with his father-in-law, started a shingle-mill—just, as he said, "to keep the boys in work." These doings for the good of Squidville made people bless the coming of Hiram Jones. Two men stood aloof from this chorus of praise—the two old guides who had loved and known Mary Weeks from her birth. It was their outspoken opinion that she was unhappy; and they pointed to the fact that she "was sickly and pale, and not caring a bit for music." Squidville folk laughed at the clattering of two old fools.

Two years had passed—years of prosperity for Hiram Jones. His parish had grown, his Endeavor Society had become a success. Spiritually he was well equipped. Materially his bank had all the choppers' money; his shingle-mill was on "the ups," as Weeks said. Weeks showed his appreciation of this by putting all his cash into the business. Squidville on its part had been faithful to its promise. It was Hiram Jones' day, and from every house they were coming in their holiday attire to do honor to their benefactor. The place of meeting was in front of Jim Weeks' hotel.

The first-comers were a little astonished to find the hotel securely locked. No amount of rapping could rouse the inmates. As the day passed the crowd grew large and uneasy. Where is Brother Jones? was the only question that seemed to take life on the lips of that motley throng. There was no one to answer.

It was growing late, and many had come from afar and were anxious to return to their homes before the coming of the dark spring night. They gathered in groups, and warmly discussed whether it was best to go home, or to break the door and "see what it all means."

In the midst of these discussions a huge mastiff dog was seen bounding and barking up the road. A hundred voices as one shouted, " Here comes Père Monnier—see his dog ! " It was true: following close to the hound was the well-known form of Père Monnier coming their way.

"Let us follow his advice," said Whistler. "I'll warrant it's a good one."

The pastor of the French-Canadian church

listened attentively to their stories. "Go," said he, addressing himself to the crowd, "and wait in the grove. I will knock at the door—Jim Weeks had always an open door for me. It was with him I lived when I first came amongst you." The crowd hurried to the grove, while Père Monnier struck the door with his cane. It was quickly opened to let him enter and as quickly shut.

Before him stood Weeks, pale and frightened, the tears running down his cheeks, his limbs quavering, and his voice hollow and broken. "O Père Monnier—Père Monnier—my old friend! I wish I were dead beside my girl—my dead Mary! Jones, the scoundrel, killed her by inches! He left a week ago and took every dollar that I had. O Père Monnier, Père Monnier!"

"She has left a little girl," said the doctor from the head of the stairs. "Mr. Weeks has given it to Mrs. La Flamme — her they call Skinny Benoit—to try and raise. Come, Skinny, and see the père."

"We will have it baptized to-morrow, père, if you see fit," said Skinny; "and I'll be true to the mother's wish, and call its first name Jenny; but as for its second name, what can it be, père? Weeks won't have it Jones."

"Call it Sauvé," said Père Monnier, entering the dead woman's room.

"Ay, père, Jenny Sauvé; *c'est beau nom* for a youngster," said Skinny.

"I'll explain all to the people," said the doctor, taking his hat.

Within lay the corpse of Mrs. Jones, Père Monnier and Jim Weeks bending over it; near to them Skinny Benoit, pressing to her bosom the new-born babe; without was a cursing, howling mob. Thus came Hiram Jones' day, to remain, as Bill Whistler said, "till Gabriel sounds the last roll-call."

CHAPTER III.

BUTTONS' LOST LOVE.

ONE July evening our boat lay at anchor in that beautiful sheet of mountain water called by the natives Round Pond, by the few fastidious New York sportsmen that annually visit it Indian Lake. We had whipped the pond from early morning,—I speak in the plural, for Billy Buttons was my guide,—and without a nibble to keep hope in expectancy. The burning sun had skin-furrowed my cheeks and pricked my flesh, while legions of singing mosquitoes had called and held their irritating conventions on the tracks old Sol had made. I was uneasy; Buttons noticed this, for he grasped the paddle and with a few quick passes brought the anchor-rope within my reach, shouting as he did so, "Doctor, pull her in." A few jerks and I landed the anchor, an awkward-looking stone, incased in black mud, in the bow.

"Where are you bound for, William?" I asked.

"For Charley Pond, doctor. There's no use in fooling any more here. The little fellows we don't want, and the big fellows ain't in the biting humor; and, what's more, fish on a tarnation hot day like this, doctor, ain't frying in the middle of the lake; they're gone up the brooks to cool. You'll find them skulking under the elders. What a tarnation day this has been, doctor. But here goes!" And Buttons, taking the oars, touched the waters, making scarcely a ripple, and away went the boat.

It may be foolish, but so beautiful was the motion of the boat under the artistic guidance of Buttons that I thought it was alive. Buttons had some like thoughts, for he said: "Doctor, I haven't much in this world, but if she [the boat] would go to pieces on one of those floating hemlocks it would be the death of me. She's as skittish as a kitten, doctor. There's no duck in these waters that can do the bowing act with her. She's a rattler, you may pin your faith to that every time. What do you think, doctor?"

I simply answered, "She's all you say. Stumps ahead, William."

"She'll dodge them by the bushel," was Buttons' assuring reply.

We had passed out of Indian Lake into a narrow channel dangerously dotted with half-burnt pine logs. The edges of this channel were lined with a scrubbish growth of dwarfish elder, "home of the foxy three-pounders," to cite Buttons' passing comment. From these elders floated long trailing, sun-burnt yellow moss, like the dishevelled hair of some village beauty. Guarding this dwarfish growth rose many a mile of stately spruce and pine, half a century ago the home of troops of yelping wolves, now the playground of the red squirrel and his lesser friend, the chattering, greedy chipmunk. This channel has two branches, one broad and deep, called the Salmon, the other gradually becoming narrower and narrower until the occupant of the boat can comfortably touch either bank with outstretched arms. This channel is difficult of access, but under the masterly skill of Buttons difficulties of this kind were converted into pleasures. Our way led by this channel. Buttons, as was his way when he scented sport, broke into song as naturally as a bird. I remember a few lines of it:

> "Chantons, chantons l'air du départ
> Nagez rameurs car l'onde fuit,
> Le rapide est proche, et le jour finit."

As an answer to this Canadian boatman's song came the quick sound of the chopper's axe, mingled with a weak human attempt to follow the lusty song of William Buttons.

"Get a hold on that twig, doc., and jerk us off that darned stump," said Buttons, rising in the boat and leaving the weary chopper to indifferently continue the song. The paddle was exchanged for an oar. "That's good, doc.; another jerk and she'll get there as sure as my name is Buttons. Ay, there she goes as straight as a pin. See how she shakes her noddle. Charley Pond, doctor—don't you see it peeping atween the bushes like a cat's eye in the dark?"

Then addressing himself to the boat: "Don't be rubbing your nose against every stump you meet, or, my pretty pet, you'll have a face on you as black as a crow's wing coming home." The boat steadied herself as if obedient to her master's will, skilfully avoided a huge log, and with a saucy skip made her first bow in Charley Pond. The little lake is wooded to the very shore with the finest specimens of spruce, tamarack, and pine. It is rimmed with soft mountain moss in many a tangled form, whose bright hues strangely mingle with the shadow of its guardian trees. A few canvasback ducks sporting in its waters eyed us long and curiously; then, with a quick wing splash and broken chatter, they rose, circled above us, stretched their necks, and, as Buttons said, "struck camp somewhere else." Our boat by this time was close to the opposite shore, about twenty feet from it, by the side of a wind-fallen pine that ran into the lake.

"Doctor," said Buttons, "get your anchor unfastened and hitch your rope to one of the branches. This is a great place for trout, if those cursed bull-pouts will go asleep and leave the bait alone. All fixed good. Why, doctor, you're the genuine stuff, what Hiram Jones used to call 'Israel's cream'; me and Cagy were the buttermilk. I'll be bound to make a fisher out of you. Throw me down the bait. How would a minny go? Give me your hook. It's baited; throw it in; no splashing—gently, doctor. By crackey! you have a bite; go easy, let him drown himself. Good! keep your line tight, he's coming on the run. Hold on; keep a stiff upper lip, doctor, and I'll get the net under him in a jiffy. Conscience, doctor, he's a beauty! a good two pounds if he's an ounce."

Encouraged by the commands and comments of Buttons, who caught trout after trout with the utmost unconcern, now and then slyly dropping one of them into my basket, I soon was in such a jovial frame of mind that my poor sick patients were forgotten, and I found myself proposing to William Buttons to build a bough shanty, and spend a few days in this most delightful retreat.

"Nonsense!" was William's reply. "If you would do that folks would think you were out of your head. They would be a-hunting and scratching for you all over the country, and of course come here. Then what would happen? Every crank in these woods would go a-fishing in Charley Pond and spoil everything. No, doctor, we'll soon get a gait on us; besides, there's a squall a-working to us. Unhitch the rope; I'll make for Dory's camp until it's over."

I never dispute the weather-knowledge of an Adirondack guide. A dark cloud passed over the lake, a few quick, sharp thunder-shots, and a serpentine ribbon of brilliant lightning skimmed the bosom of the lake as lightly as a swallow's wing. The wind rose, at first like the chattering of birds; then, grasping the pine trees and swaying their branches, sang untranslatable requiems.

The placid waters jumped, curled, and lashed

the shore, rimming the lake with creamy slobber. A few drops of rain, then a quick thunderclap, and the drops became torrents, whipping the already infuriated lake. A few frogs croaked their unmusical benisons, while we quickly pulled shoreward and hurriedly sought refuge in Dory's camp. And what a refuge!—but any port has its shelter in a storm. Dory's was a sorry sight. The roof leaked, and the wind, charged with rain, took its own way through the doorless and almost roofless camp. Buttons minded little wind or rain. "It is," he remarked, "a little summer coughing-fit, that will soon rid itself by a good rain-spit." He busied himself in making our quarters comfortable by quickly erecting, with pieces of worm-eaten boards and barked slabs, a comparatively comfortable abode. A few cracker-boxes, stuck on their end deep in the gluey mud, became chairs, while a broad board resting on our knees was a handy table. This done, "She may growl all night, doctor," said Buttons, opening a can of dried beef, while I cut a loaf with his big, long, coarse-bladed knife-of-all-work into huge pieces. An Adirondack guide wants none of your thin society bread-slices. There is a charm in puffing out the cheeks with as much bread as the mouth can hold—that is, as Cagy says, "giving play to the grinders." When Buttons was dry he pushed the table to me, went out, threw back his head, and took, as he said, "a whack at heaven's spill." It was of little account that the rain fell equally on the other parts of his face, as Buttons claimed that all the skin-furrows drained into his mouth. Every man to his taste. I admired Buttons' way of drinking, but I could not follow it; so as soon as Buttons was seated I transferred the table, upturned the beef from the can, caught some of the "spill," and took, as they say in these parts, "a long pull and a steady pull."

That pull finished one of the best meals in my life. As I sit in my office these long winter nights, penning these old memories from my diary, sickened by medicine-smells waiting for some unfortunate, what would I not give for such another meal with Billy Buttons at Dory's? Oh, Charley Pond, Dory's, heaven's spill, and Billy Buttons! somehow or other you make me sad to-night. When I was a younger man I wrote in my diary, "Glad days are sad memories." I caught that sentence one day passing Owl's Head. It came to me—broke through my headful of prescriptions. I let them go, and gleefully bagged it. I could not help saying to Toby, "I have got a good thing." Speaking even to a horse eases a fellow's mind.

"None of your pies and puddings to kick antics in my stomach after a good meal, but a good smoke and plenty of good guff," is a saying of Cagy's much quoted by Billy Buttons.

Buttons is not the man to quote a phrase and go contrary to it. While I was emptying the beef-can he unrolled his big black plug of tobacco from his deer-skin pouch, cut little bits from it, placed these in the heel of his left hand, grinding them with the knuckles of his right. This done, "Take your seat, doctor," said Buttons; "pull out your pipe and fill it: I have crushed enough for two."

No man is quicker for a pipe than I. Soon our pipes were in working order. Suddenly the smoke ceased in Buttons'; it was a way he had of being solemn. "Doctor," said he, "I'm a-thinking mighty heavy."

"What are you thinking about, William?" I asked.

"The only thing an old rounder like me thinks about—old times, old times; about the first time I came to Charley Pond, and built this camp; now it's gone to pieces. I feel for it, doctor; it seems to have something to do with me, but I can't cipher it out in talk. I feel it, just the same. It's out of 'kilter,' and I'm going the same way—that's how I size it." Buttons hung his head. I watched my pipe-smoke, and listened to the wind. Gradually Buttons' head assumed its ordinary position, and the smoke rose in his pipe. His cheeks were wet.

"I wish I was a scholar," said Buttons, drawing his glazed coat-sleeve across his face. "I would write a book."

"What would you put in it, William?" I eagerly asked. "A bear-story?"

Buttons answered angrily: "Bear-stories for New York sports — the more the better. This story is for myself, and a fellow doesn't want to fool himself with lies. It is a bit of a woman-story that has hankered around my heart a good many years; when you would hear it you would know why I brought you here."

I frankly admitted that the life of a country doctor lends itself to inquisitiveness — I believe that is the way I put it in my diary. I could not sleep without knowing that story. Would Buttons tell it? How could I start him? Buttons solved the difficulty.

"Doctor," said he, "I'm not the man to keep a story from you, and I see that the bluster outside will last while I'm telling it, so here goes: a man must have a beginning to a story. One night while I was sitting with Cagy by Jim Weeks' big office-stove swapping deer-stories, an old gentleman, a young lady, and a little girl came in. 'They're city folks,' said Cagy. I planted my eyes on them. 'So they be,' says I; 'at least they have that air about them.' 'Some of us is in for a job,' says Cagy; 'they'll surely want a guide.' Just then I heard my name called by Weeks, and over I went to his desk. 'Billy,' says he, 'don't you know that old gent that's just gone up-stairs for the night?' 'Not from Adam,' was my word. 'Why, Billy, that's queer,' said Jim. 'That's old Jenks from New York, the father of the boy that shot Skinny's husband. He wants a guide for the summer. Be ready with your kit; he'll make an early start.' 'What direction, Jim, is he pointing for?' I asked. 'He wants a quiet place,' said Jim, 'where he can build a camp and be entirely alone. His daughter is consumptive, and it is more for her sake than anything else. I have sold him our old board shanty at Charley Pond. You will soon make it slick as a new pin. Cut away all the brush. Spick her up in good shape. You'll find a scythe on the shed roof. If you need any tools you'll find them in Bill Whistler's log house a-back of the shanty.'

"Times were bad. I was glad to get a job; so I sat up all night mending my old clothes and shining my gun. By the break of day I was at the hotel. Old Jenks was ready, and away we went. It took us about six hours to get there, as in those days the little channel was more blocked than now. Berry and La Jeunesse came along to make the carries and clean out the channel. Jenks was delighted with Charley Pond. He ordered the board shanty to be pulled down, and a log cabin built in its place. We could tent until the work was done. The camp was to be called after his daughter, whose name was Dory. In a week all was ready—a regular dove's nest, and we took possession of it: Professor Jenks, his daughter Dory, the little girl Milly, and your true friend, William Buttons. It was then I began to cast my eyes around, and see in what company I was. Maybe you think I was not taken off my feet when Jenks told me that Dory was as blind as a bat—that her eyes were full of cataracts! I could hardly believe it, as her eyes looked natural, and she used to find her way through the brush. She was as handsome as a picture, doctor, and as good as God ever made. Every morning I used to watch her leaning against the trunk of a tree listening to the robins. Sometimes they would be sleepy, bobbing their little heads; then she would sing, and all at once they would shake their wings, peck their bills on the branches, and start in song. Then she would laugh — a very merry laugh at first, but the tail of it, doctor, was like the cry of a loup-garou. I have often heard the owls answer the tail of that laugh. Every day I took her on the lake, gathered fresh moss for her, baited her hook, told her stories of the voyageurs. She was a fine fisher—knew how to hold her line, and when to snap. When we came near logs she would say, ' William, where are they? How deep shall I let my line?' I would tell her, and no man that I have ever seen in these woods, with his eyes wide open, snarled his line less than Dory Jenks.

"She liked the lake in a storm. She said she could understand the ' music of water and wind-songs; that everything was full of music.' I remember how she used to sit by a little brook, with her small white hands gloved in the soft green moss, listening to its prattle, mocking its song. In those times I used to sit near her, my heart making as much noise as the brook, my eyes content—watching her every move; and some kind of a feeling, that I never had in my life before, creeping through me and making me happy. I wanted nobody around her but myself; not even Milly, who was, as Dory told me one summer night after I had sung to her guitar a little song that ends:

> ' Je n'ai ni bien, ni rang, ni gloire,
> Mais j'ai beaucoup, beaucoup d'amour,'

a New York waif taken from the streets, daughter of a drunken Spanish cigar-maker. I'll never forget that night, doctor; the sky was the color of smoke rising from the chimney on a frosty morning; one little star, about the size of a dollar, was like a gold pin stuck in a white woollen scarf. The lake was calm, trouts were jumping here and there, a crane was sleeping on a pine log, a few night-hawks were buzzing along the shore. 'It's glorious,' said Dory; 'I forget my pain. Sing, William, one of your dear old songs; I'll accompany you with my guitar.' I had many songs, but I sorted out the one with the lines I told you, because I wanted to say something I had in my heart by some other body's mouth. After the song we sat there until Milly waved a red lantern, a sign to come in. I was angry with Milly and said she knew too much for a child. 'Not so,' said Dory, 'Milly is my girl — and promise me, William Buttons, if anything happens to me and pa — of course I know it won't, but if it should — that you will befriend Milly. Just promise, William Buttons — mountain hearts keep promises — say you will, William Buttons.' I promised; she pressed my hand; a thrill of wild delight passed through me at that moment.

"Months passed away. 'Dory was,' said Professor Jenks, 'gaining strength every day, finding new life in the woods.' Daily he thanked me for my kindness to his daughter, promising to well repay all my service. His talk stabbed me. What had money to do with the services I rendered to Dory?

"The snow came one morning like a handful of flour thrown here and there on the ground and on the brush. 'It was a good day for a deer-hunt,' said Jenks. 'Bill Whistler was going out, Cagy was to meet him at the burned land; would I not take Dory in my boat and guard the pond? Dory's one wish was to shoot a deer. She would be safe with me.' 'I would lose my life for her, professor,' I replied. 'Of course you would, kind fellow; all you guides are most devoted to your parties. I shall repay you, have no fear, William; your kindness to my poor Dory will not go unrewarded,' said Jenks. My blood was boiling. Does Jenks think that I have no feelings, that I am like all the guides, that guides merely work for money?—would lose their life for it! I muttered. Jenks shouldered his gun, kissed his daughter, and started for Whistler's. I righted my boat, helped Dory to her seat, and pushed out from the shore. It was a clean-cut day; a little sharp, but just the thing for a hunt. A loud whistle told me that Whistler and Cagy had met. 'Shall we soon see a deer?' said Dory. 'That depends,' said I, 'on three things—if Cagy finds a track, if the other men miss him, and if he comes here.' 'So many ifs, William, that I fear we shall see no deer to-day,' said Dory, fingering her gun. 'Don't give up hope, Miss Jenks,' said I; 'Cagy knows I am here, and unless he's changed a good deal Mr. Deer will have to visit William Buttons.' 'Hark! don't you hear a hound away off?' said Dory, looking in the direction of the sound. 'I do, Miss Jenks,' says I; 'it's Cagy's dog, Mickey.' 'What music he makes! the whole woods are filled with his voice, noble animal—now he stops!' said Dory. 'They are in the swamp, Miss Jenks; the deer is circling; there he goes—hear the dog coming this way? You will soon hear some shooting—that is, if they are on the right runaways.' 'I don't hear the dog, William—I do hope he will bring him here,' said Dory, moving restlessly in her seat. 'Hear him now, Miss Jenks? That deer never was born that could lose Cagy's dog; he lost him in the poplars, but it was only for a minute. Listen! the deer is taking a sweep; the dog will hang to him, he's bound to water him, trust Billy Buttons — Cagy would shoot a dog that would give up his deer. Bang, bang—six shots —they didn't get him—too many cracks. Miss Jenks, he's coming on the dead run for Charley Pond. Keep quiet and he'll get more than he bargained for.' The word was no sooner out of my mouth than a huge buck came to the edge of the lake, stood for a moment with pointed ears listening to the coming dog, shot his eyes around the lake, plunged in and swam for the opposite shore. It was but the work of a moment to cut off his retreat by getting between him and the shore. He saw this — deers are no fools; his eyes flashed like lanterns in the woods in a dark night, his body was all nerves, and, turning on his back track, he was making for the shore. One glance was enough; the dog had come to the lake, savagely growled, closely scanned the water, and saw a moving spot. He was too old in the business not to know what that meant—a lively bark to warn his master that his prey was secure, a dance of joy, a plunge, and Cagy's dog, the best that ever put foot to clay, was swimming towards him. Now was the time. I came as close to Dory in the boat as was prudent for our safety, and, stretching my right hand, guided the barrel of her gun. The deer was but a rod from us. 'Shoot,' I cried, and the sharp, pleasant clang of the Winchester rang over the lake and went a-rambling in the woods. A sharp cry from Dory and, quicker than I speak, our boat was struck by the deer's antlers, capsized, and Dory and I in the lake. My first thought was of her; there she was struggling for life, ready to sink. I quickly grasped her, held up her head, and, with a few strokes, brought her ashore.

"Whistler, Cagy, and her father had returned; they heard my story, sent for Mrs. Whistler, tried every means to revive her, but "—a tear started in Buttons' eye—" she died in two hours after, doctor. Just before she died she opened her mouth just a little bit and said: 'Charley.' That word, doctor, made me stagger. I wanted her to speak again, but it was not to be.

"We buried her in Squidville graveyard, just under the big white beech tree; it was my way. Her poor old father had lost his mind and could not give an order about the grave. Weeks took him to New York; that was the last I heard of him. The beech tree—yes, I picked that place out just because I thought of how she used to lean against the trees and listen to the birds' songs. It is the biggest tree in the graveyard, and singing birds, doctor, like big trees—they want a height when they pitch their voices. I planted rose trees, but they died for want of sun—the big beech would have no other mate in guarding Dory's grave. Years after, when in Montreal, I bought a piece of marble, made them cut on it 'Charley,' and put it at the head of Dory's grave. People thought it was strange, so may you; but that matters little. I always say that strange things are only strange to those who don't understand them.

"That's my story. That's why I am here,

brought by a fading memory. Dory's camp is a ruin, and I, Billy Buttons — but no use in complaining; life is rather short for that. Fill your pipe, doctor, and let us go; that rain-spit is over."

We righted the boat and pulled out. The lake was calm, the ducks had returned, the moss was arrayed in a bridal dress of slobber, a robin from a tall pine sang us a parting song. Out of Charley Pond and down the narrow channel glided our little boat, Buttons smoking and thinking mighty heavy, the country doctor impatient to pen an old guide's story.

CHAPTER IV.

THE COMING OF SLITHERS.

It was after a lucky bear-hunt that Professor Clark, startled by the wonderful knowledge of his Adirondack guides, declared that " the natural intelligence of Squidville's children should be quickened by education. To show you," continued the professor, " that I am in dead earnest in this matter I will donate the sum of one hundred dollars,—yes, one hundred,—and that at once, as a starter."

Cagy drank in the professor's words, and under the pretext of " Provisions out, sir," left the camp that night with basket and rifle for the Hunter's Paradise. The basket was to be filled with canned goods, and the rifle to be handy in case of an odd shot.

Cagy communed with himself on the way. He had often heard sportsmen when talking of this or that guide say: " The greatest pity in the world the poor fellow can neither read nor write."

" The same," thought Cagy, " would be said

of the rising folk if they didn't get a chance."
Now was the time—he would see Billy Buttons,
and if he thought it was right, then they would
lay before Weeks what Clark had said, neither
cutting it shorter nor making it longer.

Cagy, by near cuts only known to the trained
guide, was soon in sight of Buttons' log cabin.
The little Poulets sat in front of the door, for
William had captured the widow and her brood.

An Adirondack guide is long-winded when his
subject is a hunt. Then he recognizes that
he is an artist and must carefully produce each
shade of his masterpiece. On other subjects,
and especially with his fellows, he bags his game
with the first shot. Cagy lost no words with
Buttons, and with the swarm of young Poulets
on hand Buttons was right glad to second the
motion that "Jim be informed of the offer of
the finest man that ever struck the woods." It
was but a step to Weeks', and the two old
chums made it a lively one.

They were welcomed by Weeks' giant hand-
shake and hearty voice: "Boys, what's up?
Something worth scratching for, I'll warrant."

To Weeks' question Cagy answered by cross-
ing his lips—a mountain sign that means, "Folks
around and leakage in them."

Telling his boy-of-all-work, Frank La Flamme, to fill Cagy's basket, he invited the guides to his barn, promising them something worth seeing—the best colt from here to Snipeville. Once in secrecy, Cagy's message was quickly laid before him, with Buttons' often-repeated comment that "A school would be the making of Squidville for now and forever."

"Cagy, you're what I call a genuine corker; you're always thinking of other folks — one of those lads that sees ahead. I have no family; I had,"—Buttons and Cagy turned their heads,—"but I am for the good of Squidville every time; so I'll go the professor a hundred."

"Thank you, Jim Weeks," said Cagy, "and if you'll be so kind as to keep out of my monthly check ten dollars, just to keep the ball a-hopping, I'll be more than obliged."

There was a tear in Buttons' eye as he stammered out: "Changed times with Billy Buttons; put me down for five."

"Is marriage a failure, Billy?" said Weeks, laying his finger-tips kindly on Buttons' shoulder.

"No, Jim; since I come by the Poulets I'm as happy as a lark, but when a fellow has so many bills pecking at what he brings in—not that I begrudge anything to my wife or the children of Tom Poulet—he cannot be as free as he would wish."

"Your five is better than my hundred," said Weeks; "it is harder for you to spare it."

Cagy scratched his head; his face wore a troubled expression. "Jim Weeks," said he, "take another five from my wages and put it along with Buttons' as an evener; what's mine is Billy's. If I was dying to-morrow I would make for Billy's."

"My house is yours, and the latch-string is out for you by day and night, whenever you're around," said Buttons, grasping his friend's hand.

"I know it, old man, I know it," said Cagy. "You and Jim will see to things. I must be making for the camp."

Next day at the dinner-hour Billy Buttons, accompanied by young La Flamme lustily ringing Jim Weeks' dinner-bell, made a tour of Squidville. It was a way of telling folk "that something was a-coming to a head." On his return he stopped at every house and sang:

>   "To-night or never
>   Lost forever,
>   A school.
> Come one, come all,
> To Jim Weeks'. Oh, oh, oh!"

The prolonged "Oh!" was musically supported by the timely ringing of La Flamme's bell. Squidville had so few excitements that fall that it gladly listened to William's voice.

There is no appointed hour in these parts to open a meeting. It is our way to begin when the hall is well filled. That night by seven, a decent hour, it was overflowing. Jim Weeks, amid applause, was made chairman. He excused himself for not sitting, preferring to lean against a cracker-barrel the better to study their faces. His speech was allowed on all hands to have been a rip-snorter. He stopped at nothing. He cited the Bible, and what some big city gun had told him in confidence. When he came to say: "We are Americans; Squidville is in New York, and every loon knows that New York is in America, therefore Squidville folks are Americans, and it is the right of every American to have an education," the audience went wild.

"I wouldn't miss that for all I'm worth," was the ordinary comment.

Bill Whistler, just as the meeting was going to take names and their contributions, asked privilege to say a few words. It was granted. "Fellow-taxpayers," said he, "our burdens are—"

There was a shuffling of feet and a craning of necks.

"I move that Whistler turns off his gas," said Buttons.

"Second the motion," said La Jeunesse.

"He's not in it with you, Jim," said Berry.

"He's talking through his hat," said Brie.

"I'll ring the changes on him," said La Flamme, vigorously shaking his bell.

"This is coming to be a pandimion, and you know what Gliggins said about pandimions," shouted a female voice from the crowd.

"Boys!" shouted Weeks, "here's the point: will we let our young folks grow up like a lot of woodchucks, just know enough to carry them around, for the sake of a few miserable dollars in the way of taxes? or will we make men of them, and put some of them on the road to be senators? Just think of it, boys—me calling one of the youngsters Senator Whistler, Senator Poulet; that's the way, as Jenks used to say, 'to cast your optics on a thing.'"

Weeks had conquered. Bill Whistler yielded to his spell. "Ay," said he, "true; I should have looked at it by Jim's way. My Johnny or Zebediah might be senators, exactly. I am a great man for discussion. Last week's *Pioneer* said: 'Let there be discussion; everything above-board; the man that provokes discussion is a benefactor.' Now, boys, you'll have to give me credit for getting that last corker of an argument out of Jim."

The meeting was a great success. Enough money was contributed to build a district school and keep it in fuel for two winters. Weeks gave the building-lot, and became the first trustee. It was a new and strange duty, but he was not the man to flinch from a trust. A few weeks later the first page of the *Porcupine Pioneer* contained the following notice:

"HUNTER'S PARADISE.

"*Best Summer Board in the Adirondacks.*

"To all whom it may concern: I, James Weeks, being duly appointed trustee of Squidville school by a meeting of taxpayers called for that purpose, do hereby notify teachers that I am on the lookout for one of them, provided the same comes up to my notion of what is wanted. Petitioners must be gentlemen, Christians, and scholars. No bad habits. Must have a good 'commend' from former boss.

"Notay Bainaz.

"All Petitioners must bring their characters along with them."

This advertisement was handsomely supported by an editorial pointedly headed, "To Be or

Not to Be: That's the Question." In this editorial were shown the labors of Weeks in behalf of education, and an advice to its readers — that the right man would be well treated.

This appeal was answered in person by a man of thirty, tall and slim, bulging forehead, cat-eyes steel-gray; pointed nose, thin lips, and retreating chin. His voice, as Sal Purdy said, was the only thing pretty about him. That, she declared, was "as sweet as syrup." He wore a black suit of ministerial cut, kid gloves, beaver hat, a little shiny and tilted to one side. His right hand held an umbrella much the worse for wear. He carried a little satchel in his left hand, containing his "recommends." As he came by the stage, it gave Squidville a chance of seeing him. Every house was crowded with eager faces to get a peep at the man of learning. It was the general say that he was something out of the run, and the hope was expressed that Weeks would see his way "to let him have the school." Berry had taken an interest in the stranger. As the stage halted in front of the Hunter's Paradise he grasped the professor's hand, warning him that the prettiest way to come at Jim was to keep his tongue from wabbling and allow Jim to do the talking.

The stranger thanked the stage-driver for his sage advice, and, taking his belongings, waited on Squidville's trustee. Buttons gave the professor the only arm-chair. La Flamme ran to tell his master that " one of the city folk was come."

" How do? Just got here?" was Weeks' salutation.

The professor rose, put his umbrella on the counter, his bag on the chair, pulled from his vest-pocket his eyeglasses, wiped them with a faded handkerchief extracted from his coat-tail pocket, and calmly placed them on his nose.

A profound impression sat on Buttons' face.

" My health, sir!" said the man of learning, " is of the best—at its acme, if I may say so. I am in splendid form for a scholar. I have got rid of waste tissue, that clog of all true scholars. And here I may state that, reading in the *Porcupine* your most healthy epistle to the teaching brethren, I bethought of offering my services as preceptor—*magister*, as we say in the Latin tongue—to an institution that shall perpetuate your name and fame, not only to the rising generations, but, as a scholar would put it, *per omnia sæcula sæculorum*."

The final sentence was too much for Buttons. Jumping from his seat, he exclaimed: "Professor, you're a whole luminary in yourself. Why, Jim, that's mighty powerful speaking. If only the Poulets knew how to speak that last language I would die like a seigneur. Père Monnier's the only man I ever heard speaking those same words, and the only difference is that he uses his hands more."

"The Poulets may learn it if I am retained," said the stranger. "My ambition will be to train a race of Americans that shall love their God and their country, and willingly die for both; men"—and the professor waxed warm—"whose brave hearts shall throb to the siren strings of humanity." Here he remembered Berry's advice, removed his bag, and meekly sat down.

"Show me your commends," said Weeks.

A smile played on Buttons' face as he said: "I'll warrant he's chock-full of them."

"Quality, William Buttons, not quantity, counts," said Weeks.

"That is most excellently put," said the professor; "a magnificent example of conciseness."

The little bag was quietly opened, and a

huge bundle of papers, faded and fresh leaves, neatly spread on the counter.

"These," said the smiling stranger, "are but a few."

"My heavens!" said Buttons, "only a few; if you have any more you have the longest character of any man of my acquaintance."

Weeks patiently read letter after letter—at least he spent some time on every sheet. An old yellow leaf, roughly scrawled, held him. "Listen, Billy! On account of this commend I give the care of Squidville school, at eight dollars per week,—am I understood pertinently and distinctly?—to Corkey Slithers, here present, to have and to hold for the natural term of one year."

Corkey rose, bowed, saying: "Mr. Trustee, you are, sir, distinctly, pertinently understood, and your offer accepted, by Corkey Slithers." Buttons shook the professor's hand.

Weeks read in a loud, stumbling voice from the yellow leaf:

"Corkey Slithers, Esq.,

well known to me, who knew him since he wasn't the hight of your nee, asks for a commend, and I give it this very minit. Corkey is an Americin, true blew at that, who belives that the poorest should have an

edukashun eqal to the rich. He's a worker from away back, a man of the people.
"Yours,
"MR. TATTERS MCGARVEY,
"*Constitution House, Snipeville.*"

"That's an honest letter," said Weeks, carefully folding it; "none of your nonsense about Tatters."

"Exactly," said the professor; "he overspells in some places, but it was not for its spelling, but for its honesty, that I laid it before you, Mr. Trustee."

"It's hard, Mr. Slithers," said Weeks, "for an old dog to learn new tricks. When we were young, Tatters and I, there were neither schools nor school-masters. What we have in our skulls is but pickin's gathered here and there. We know our want, and don't wish the children to be like us in that respect. In honesty and kindness we have no masters. You have had a long, rough ride, professor, and must be hungry. It's dinner-time. Ring the bell, Frankie; come along with us, Buttons, and make no excuses."

"Well, by jingo, that's as tidy as my boat," said Buttons as La Jeunesse drove the last nail in the saddle-boards of Squidville's school.

A crowd had gathered "to see her finished, done up in good style."

To William's outburst came their contented cry, "Yes, by jingo, she's all you say, and more."

La Jeunesse ran down the ladder like a cat; Weeks threw up his hat; the professor took a side-squint at his academy; Frankie rang the bell; and Cagy's fellow-guides, from Snipeville and Porcupine Creek, sang:

> "We won't go home till morning,
> We won't go home till morning—
> Till daylight does appear."

Seeing folk make so merry, a bright idea came to Weeks. Running to the Hunter's Paradise, astonishing everybody by his agility, he wrote a notice, and, coming as quickly as he had gone, nailed it to the door. It read:

"At 7 P.M. sharp a meeting of praise and thanks will be held in this school-house. All invited. Bring chairs; benches put in next week. First appearance of Professor Slithers in his capacity of Principal. Friends of education turn out, and show the people of the surrounding towns that you are no back-sliders. Astonish Mr. Corkey by what the *Pioneer* calls 'our exuberance.' A fee of ten cents at the door, to buy books for the orphans. Long live Squidville, and hip, hurrah, boys, for Corkey Slithers!

"JIM WEEKS, *Trustee*."

Milly De La Rosa, a pretty miss of seventeen, was called on by the happy crowd to "cipher out what Jim Weeks was up to." Milly was the village pet.

"Don't be afraid," said Buttons in a fatherly way, "Milly; you're ciphering it out first rate."

"Loud, black-eyes!" said Weeks, "or I'll make Frankie stay in the store to-night." Milly blushed.

"Go on, child," said the delighted Cagy; "it's astonishing how you get around Weeks' lingo. You're as smart as a steel trap, and Corkey will polish you off like a diamond."

"That's all," said Milly, with a saucy shake of the head.

"Bravo!" shouted the crowd. "Untutored children," said the professor; "what a rich soil to sow in the immortal seeds of education!"

"You struck bottom that time," said Buttons; "it's in them every time for the taking out. They're as quick as chain-lightning."

"Naked truth, Buttons," said Whistler: "just the stuff to make your senators."

"You bet," says Berry, "and they wouldn't

blather away in Washington and let the country go to shocks."

Frankie rang his bell. Weeks and the professor started for the Hunter's Paradise, followed by the crowd singing.

At seven the school-house was filled, and Chairman Weeks had called the meeting to order. His remarks, as I find them in the *Pioneer*, were that Education makes the man, the want of it the fellow; that he felt its loss in every step of life. That the best thing a man could do for his country was to help to educate his fellow-men. For this reason the orphan lad that he had brought up as his own child, the son of poor Napoleon La Flamme, would be placed under the care of his friend Professor Slithers, and he hoped that all parents and guardians of children would follow his example.

The speech of Professor Slithers I take from the same journal:

"*Libertas et natale solum*, as we say in the Latin tongue. Friends, that is a sentiment to be profoundly cherished. How shall we cherish it? By giving our sons and daughters, in the words of our distinguished chairman, an education."

Here there is a break, as there was not space

in the first page of the *Pioneer* to insert the whole speech. In the advertising part of the same paper you will find the wind-up, which took Squidville by storm. I copy it:

"Education is liberty. Liberty shall never die. Slavery is Carthage; and as the Latins say, *Delenda est Carthago*. When the rotten governments of Europe are sunk in the ocean, when not a vestige of the earth shall remain, Liberty, as represented by our Eagle, shall on the highest pinnacle of the Rockies stand, spread her tail-feathers, kick out her hind leg in derision, and say Boo! to the rest of the world. These, O men of Squidville! be the undying sentiments of Slithers."

Such sentiments won him the heart of Squidville town, and the promise by the morrow of seventy "regular scholars." No wonder that Weeks said: "Professor Clark, may heaven be your bed, for what you have done for us!" And Jemmie Barbier, the village patriarch and guardian of Milly De La Rosa: "It's hard for my old wife to spare Milly, but we must make a little sacrifice in this world, and to what you say, Jim Weeks, I say Amen, and add, May heaven be your bed!"

CHAPTER V.

THE WOOING OF MILLY.

The election was over; the party of Pink had won, congratulations were hearty. "The people's will had triumphed. Popular government had been vindicated," said the solitary leader in the *Porcupine Pioneer*, hemmed in between a crowing rooster and Old Glory.

Bill Whistler had other ideas, standing on Weeks' piazza and looking at the half-drunken voters with right hands in their trousers pockets firmly clutching the two-dollar bills, "the ordinary price of votes in these parts," he was heard to remark; "the people's will and popular government are catchwords that mean nothing. The drunken fellows don't know what they are voting for. You have filled them with whiskey, put their price in their hands, told them to vote; they have done so, and now you have the hardihood to call this the people's will, popular government."

"Bill," said Berry, whose stage had carried the colors of Punk, "no use in talking. Pink had the most money and the most whiskey; that's what sweeps the stakes."

"We ain't to blame," said a staggering voter; "it's the Church-folk—the best pickings at that, these temperance fellows—who sent us the whiskey."

"Strange thing," said Ike Perkins, "that they preach temperance every day in the year but election-day. About their whole concern on that day is to make drunkards."

"That's a fact, Ike. Yet the election of Pink is, according to the *Pioneer*, the people's will, vindication of popular government," was Whistler's last shot at the triumphant party approaching the Hunter's Paradise. Pink, smiling, shaking hands with every man he met, telling jokes of Squidville prepared for the day, was escorted to the private room and closeted with Jim Weeks.

The outcome of this secret meeting was that Squidville was to have a post-office with full connections with Snipeville. Weeks was ever mindful of his friends.

On Pink's memorandum-book, slated for Squidville's first post-master, was the name of

William Buttons. "He has married into a houseful of Poulets, is getting old, and for what he was deserves the office. With Buttons as post-master, and Cagy running the Snipeville stage, the mail is bound to get there," was Weeks' exultant word.

Pink closed his memorandum-book, and in a knowing way pressed Weeks' hand. Teams were in readiness; Pink's party drove forth amid yells and human imitations of cock-crowing. Whistler sauntered home with a showy contempt for the drunken men that had betrayed their party. Little groups lingered in the Hunter's Paradise telling of the things that had happened until Weeks, tired of his day's work, shouted, "Time to close; all home; your wives will think that you're lost."

With a "Don't trouble yourself about that, Jim," the merry groups went home. Night fell on the mountain town. La Flamme's dogs warned a yelping fox to retreat.

Billy Buttons said to his wife, "There's music in Squidville to-night." "There may be more by the morrow," was the sleepy reply.

It was so. He was sleeping, dreaming of deer and Charley Pond, when his door was pounded to the tune of ringing laughter. He arose, hurriedly dressed, and opening the door found himself in the arms of Jim Weeks.

While Bill Whistler congratulated him on being post-master from that very minute, with power to name the man who should carry the mail between his town and Snipeville, Buttons, for the first time in his life, "became," as Cagy remarked, "so rattled that he couldn't draw a tricker." It passed. He was no speech-maker, but like all guides in a moment when dumbness might mean ingratitude his tongue was thawed.

"Boys," said he, "you are all corkers. I wish I was Slithers, to tell you all I feel. To be the first post-master of Squidville is no small honor; I know that, and my only thought will be to please you. I'm no scholar; but my stepson Poulet — I'm only saying what Slithers says — can read anything on paper. I'll do my best, boys, and you'll all help me."

"You ought to be pretty certain of that, Billy," was their joint reply.

"Boys, I have known it for thirty years," was his answer.

"Post-master Buttons, who will run the Snipeville stage?" said Weeks in a bantering way.

"I don't want to be too bossy at first, Jim;

but if you left it to me Cagy, the best fellow in the world, should have it," said Buttons.

"Struck the mark!" said Weeks. "Heavens, what a team they'll make!" said Andrieux. "Cagy's fixed for life!" said Whistler. "What a pair of steppers!" shouted Brie. "They're as good as they make them," said Berry. Cagy clasped Buttons' hand, while the well-wishers went to their daily employment.

Mrs. Buttons was right. "There was more music in the morning." The young Poulets, carried away by the importance that had come to stay in their family, opened their throats and sent forth a volume of sound, making Professor Slithers remark, "Menagerie on fire?"

The remainder of the day was spent by the two old guides looking for a suitable building to carry on "the lettering business." Towards evening a bargain was had of a frame house on the banks of the Salmon River, largely dilapidated, but, as Cagy remarked, "easy to right." It was considered spacious, a point of note in a country post-office.

"I'll put up my stand here," said Buttons, lounging in a corner of the house. "I'll have a desk, a few forms for the boys to sit on."

"It would be a first-class idea to put the

box-stove in the middle of the floor," said Cagy; "it would give the boys more room to kick."

"Right you are, Cagy; I'll have no cooping business in my office."

"I have a thought, Billy, that you ought to square off the other corner for a store."

"That same idea, Cagy, is hatching in my skull. Folks, when they come for letters, will be willing to take home a few groceries under their arm. A post-office is no great shakes as a money-maker. It's only as a feeder to a store that it counts."

"One thing, Billy, you must not forget, and that's to gouge a good hole in the door, for polite folk who won't come in to pass through their mail."

"It's a mighty queer way for folk," said Buttons, "even if they are on the ups, to think that a post-master has nothing else to do but stand behind a door waiting to see a letter shoot through."

"You're shooting high, Billy. My meaning is, after you gouge the hole, to put a box behind it, what Mr. Corkey would call a receiver. There's no need then to be standing behind the door. Go about your business. As soon as the letter is sent scooting it will take a drop, and be there until you pick it up."

"Why, Cagy," said the delighted Buttons, "that's as clear as spring-water with a sandy bottom. A fellow in my business has to put up with all kinds of folk. I'll follow your plan, though, there's no mistake about it, in a free country like this I think everybody should come right up to the counter and do their business open."

"Free country, Billy, has nothing to do with it. It's all nature, and she's a lassie' pretty hard to twist. You cannot make woodchucks run like foxes, or ducks trot like hens. Take folks as they be and hold your reins accordingly."

"It's a fact, Cagy. It's time to go. Pull the door after you; as soon as I am rigged I'll have to put a lock on the door. It seems all so funny, these new lifts in life, don't it, Cagy?—so funny to leave the woods and all our bearings. With the help of God I won't part with my gun and dog. I'll have a whack at the deer this fall."

"Billy," said Cagy mournfully, "if we are going into the government business it doesn't mean that we are going to give up our liberty.

By deer-time the Poulets will be able to run the office tip-top, and Brie can take my place, so we'll be able to do the right thing by the deer. Anyway, it wouldn't make much fuss if the letters were three or four weeks later; news don't spoil."

Two old guides went laughing down Pleasant View. Three months passed before the necessary papers came from Washington. When they came it was known to Squidville. Berry announced the news from his passing stage. "Boys, hurrah! the senator's made Buttons a post-master without a whimper. I have all the papers." He had. They were addressed to Jim Weeks.

A crowd gathered at the Hunter's Paradise to hear the "latest." Weeks, opening the bulky envelope, from the piazza addressed them: "This is a bright day for us. We're in it with the rest of the country. We have churches, school, and now, to crown everything, a post-office. Your loves and sorrows will be attended to now. The half of you can sell your horses, seeing business is so easy. Give your letters to friend Buttons; he'll see that they make a good start. You have only to write. Buttons, as soon as he is able, will sell everything in his line. Show your spunk by writing to all your friends, and help Billy. He's only allowed what stamps he crosses. Give him enough. You'll find him in at eight to-morrow; give him a call."

This speech of Jim's was received with cheers. It was the general say that a stiff business in letter-writing would be done that day. To the honor of local patriotism be it written that men and women hunted up lost uncles and distant cousins in order to show their appreciation of William Buttons. Professor Slithers gave half a day to his scholars in order to direct the huge bundle of letters for the morning's mail. Cagy busied himself with the rigging of the Snipeville stage. It was to start at nine, returning the next evening at three, meeting Berry at Squidville; transferring passengers there for Porcupine Creek, Mud Pond, Duck Lake, Otter Bend, and all points south. Snipeville was to give a supper. Tatters McGarvey, Esq., was to make a speech and Cagy was down to reply. It was the trial of his life. As he rigged his stage he made his speech, violently shaking the wheels when he scored a point, surlily scratching his head when he missed the mark.

Not since the days when the doctor announced

the flight of Hiram Jones was there such a commotion in Squidville. "It is," said Bill Whistler, "my idea of a popular demonstration."

Commotion, like a dry-bough fire, soon subsides. People are limited on every subject. After Weeks' speech had been viewed from every point bed was refreshing. Tongues tire, eyes shut of their own accord, and heads become heavy. Sleep, whispering of the great things of the morrow, tickled the Squidvillites. They bent to her sway. La Flamme's dogs kept watch. Afar away a fox now and then sent them a note of defiance. A deer under the cover of night crossed the river. A catamount hung on the edge of the mountain. The dogs laughed at such insolence: they, too, were dreaming of the morrow. Squidville slept. It is easy to tell when a mountain town awakes. A slight thread of smoke peeps from a chimney, curling itself into light gray rings, dying in the arms of the cool mountain breeze. Other chimneys follow, doors creak on rusty hinges, pent-up dogs salute their fellows, cows bellow, calves become frisky, and folks are busy doing "chores."

"What a life!" says the sallow, thin-blooded

sportsman as he turns in his bed, pulls the chair near that holds his vest, extracts his watch just marking five. He turns on the other side, smiles at his fellows, hears the jingle of gold in the dropped vest, consoles himself, and goes to sleep.

"What a scarecrow that sport is!" says the guide later.

"As sallow as a duck's foot; a few crooked bones rolled in parchment, and making a poor parcel at that. He's as full of disease as an egg's full of meat," says another, "and as shrivelled as a beech leaf out all winter."

"He's bound to snap. There's no sap in him," says a third.

"I wouldn't be in his boots for all the money in the world," says a fourth.

It's our way to criticise each other. Happiness is many-sided. It is consoling to have such a word in the dictionary as opinion.

Buttons' chimney led Squidville in the morning. It was closely followed by Weeks'. "I'm going over to Jim's for instructions," was Buttons' parting words to his wife. Early as it was the Hunter's Paradise was open, and young La Flamme so intent on writing that Buttons had to slap him on the shoulders to make him aware of his presence. "Hello, Billy! ain't you early up?" was his word. "Not a bit more than you be," was Buttons' retort.

"Do you open your office at eight, Billy?"

"Well, yes, Frank, that is the intention — to have the mail made up for Cagy to have a good start."

"It's rather early, Billy. There's no sense in shutting up at three and opening at eight. The time between is just when a fellow has a chance to skip out and post his letter."

"Young man," said Buttons with an air of authority, "government business is not like running a hotel: it has its hours. You're at everybody's hour. I'm a government servant. As to your talk about shutting up, it shows how little you know about government business. There is no shut up, no such thing as a still post-office. I have put in a receiver; if I'm out he's in."

"A receiver, Billy! Who is he?"

"There you are again, youngster; you have been to Slithers' school for a year, and you don't know what a receiver is. It doesn't argue for a long head. In the door I've gouged a hole big enough for a decent-sized envelope to slide through. Push it until it takes a drop.

Of course it is only for gentle folk; but I suppose you're like all the youngsters: you'll be cock of the roost or nothing."

"Good-morning, post-master!" said the hearty Weeks, opening a side door. "Go to your breakfast, Frankie."

The boy's face lighted up; bounding from the store, he followed a path that soon brought him, unnoticed, to the post-office. The gouged hole made him dance with delight.

"Buttons never picked that out of his own head," he shouted. "Just the thing. I can write to Milly, and no one will be the wiser." His heart beat faster; his heart was wound up in that delicious name. "I don't see why Jemmie Barbier went to Snipeville to live. Milly didn't like it a bit. I can't bear that Slithers. He thought, because he was her teacher, that he would cut me out. He can write better than me, has more in his head to work on; but if she likes me the best she won't pay much attention to the writing; it's what's in it that counts. Cagy will work for me. She'll visit my mother and make friends with Jenny. They'll work for me. Everybody is on my side. Anyhow, I don't see how she can like that horrid Corkey."

These broken mutterings were consoling. La Flamme put his letter in the receiver, laughed at its pleasant dropping sound, and, taking the same path, gleefully ran to the Hunter's Paradise. A few hours after the post-office was opened for business, the Snipeville stage before the door, and a brisk business for Buttons. The people had shown their spunk. A late caller was Professor Slithers, who had left his school in charge of the largest girl. His thoughts were of Milly De La Rosa.

"How romantic her history!" he was saying. "Daughter of Castile mated to Corkey Slithers, ha, ha! I know my poem, when she reads it, will take her. What a capital idea is poetry! Things you cannot think of saying in prose, how easy they go in verse! What a fine beginning is the opening line:

'Enchantress of Castile'!

Then, showing the power she has concentrated on the seat of my affections, I remark:

'I bend beneath thy heel.'

If this is not poetry, then all the poetry in the Recent Collection of American Verse is unmitigated prose. That poem is my bait, so tempting that, once drawn in the line of her swimming, she'll hook."

Reflections such as these steadied his nerves and brought victory nodding to him. He was soon in sight of the office. The Snipeville stage had left — a fact that made his pleasant thoughts sour. The door was shut — additional evidence "of the way things were run." Within was a laughing crowd listening to Buttons' inimitable wood-tales. Sourness dislikes pleasantry. He was on his heel to return when the rough, awkward mouth of the receiver caught his eye. A wave of joy passed through him. The effect was visible in his eyes and a wriggling in his left foot. Taking his letter, pursy and unpressed, he squeezed it through the opening. The drop was music. It was a day's thought, a pretty story. The opening chapter in Squidville, the grand finale in Snipeville. The last act was a hooked fish. All of us have theatres pretty thoroughly rigged. Buttons stopped his tale to remark that the professor was of the gentle folk.

There was a smile, a shuffling of feet, and the story became more interesting. The professor was on his return. His brain-puppets were in scene first, act the second. It represented William Buttons extracting from the receiver a letter addressed to Milly De La Rosa, containing intentions of love, and a poem after the manner of a Recent Collection of Verse. The actor that represented William seemed puzzled at the handwriting, and was saying to Cagy: "I wonder who writes to Milly; I'll bet that letter's worth having." "It wouldn't be Mr. Corkey?" responds Cagy. "A happy day for Milly to be mated to such a man," is Buttons' remark. Cagy puts the letter into the Snipeville bag with an air of importance, and the curtain drops.

Weeks passed; the general verdict was that Buttons had shown himself equal to his post. Harmony would make the world tasteless. Growlers are the salt of the earth. There were two in Squidville. Milly had not written, and Buttons' office was denounced by Slithers as an absurdity; in the more expressive vocabulary of La Flamme, as a worn-out fake. Such expressions were perplexing. If Milly would not write, why blame Buttons? It is not commendable to commit forgery. How else could William have given letters to his eye-devouring callers? Cagy was slyly questioned. He kept the saddle by an aphorism: "You cannot tell what you don't know." Plants grow towards the sun; love to its object. Letters were to be the rays. Shut off, love and plants languish. It takes time to kill them. Give them sunshine in the drooping state, and they will quickly revive. Months had passed. Slithers, unconsolable at first, was adjusting his sorrow. It was not the first time he had balanced his books.

La Flamme became sick and lonely. The store was a nuisance, friends a bother. Life was full of blue streaks, sleep a friend. In church he made a mental vow never to believe a woman's word. He did not express it, but the idea was constant in his mind that woman was created, much as the mountain brier, to tear men's flesh. The thought bothered him, as it awoke another, that these briers gave fruit. At this he forgot himself and muttered: "Love! Yes, but you must tear yourself to pluck it." His mutterings made a charitable friend in a back pew elbow him. He was in a mood to resent. His eyes did the fighting. It was during the battle of glances that Père Monnier, in his artless way, said: " To accomplish anything in this life requires sacrifice." The rest of the sermon was forgotten; this was a limb pulled from the tree to cudgel the blue streaks. His love for Père Monnier was great from that day.

La Flamme was of that great company of sinners who pick a line from a sermon and label it, "Meant for me." The sentence fitted his mood. It became his pocket-pistol through life. With it he shot sorrow, and, let us hope, kept the way open to the better land.

Buttons had a keen ear for sound. The sayings of Slithers and La Flamme nettled him. He would have made them chew their words had he not learned at Charley Pond that love made men queer. Like all guides, he leaned on the past. Pitying their condition, he asked Cagy to find out "a something of Milly." A day later Cagy's information was poured into his ears, prefaced by a remark that Milly had no right to marry out of Squidville. The information was scanty, but prickly. It spoke of Slithers as "an educated fool," of La Flamme as "an ungratefull wretch." The terms were strong.

The information came from Milly. Rumor added that she was engaged. This news leaked, and Squidville had its laugh. "Corkey was jilted, La Flamme was crazy," was the way it was put Corkey from past battles learned to laugh; La Flamme keenly felt the sore, but cheered himself by shooting the spectre with his pocket-pistol. Cagy was proud of him. "His father every time," he said: "under fire he won't flinch."

In the way Milly had said "ungrateful wretch" the old guide, so accustomed to study faces, read hope. "Come with me, Frankie," he said. "I'll never go back on your father's son. You'll have a free ride, and you have a fine excuse. Tell Weeks you want to see your mother and Jenny. I have found the track, and the deer is not so far but we can run her down. Once she hears your music, and knows you are in dead earnest, I don't think she'll run far."

La Flamme listened. Had he followed his first thought he would have started. Reflection made him a coward. It began with an if, allowed the conclusion; started another if, allowed its conclusion. Soon he had a bundle of them. The end of the play represented him leaving Snipeville in disgrace: Milly and her lover, heads closely pressed behind a window, making fun of him. He admitted his cowardice, was downed by a brain-figment. He had forgotten his pocket-pistol. Cagy started. La Flamme bade him a wistful good-bye. They prate of love, that it conquers all things. Sarcasm has often dulled its edge. "He who waits will be rewarded," is a stock phrase, used as a trotter by the well-to-do. It is not much in vogue with the waiter. Like most stock phrases, an accident may give it a meaning.

A year had passed. Slithers, despite the village talk, had continued to woo the muses as meshes for entangling Milly. La Flamme had daily fed Buttons' receiver with letters. Milly was dead to such appeals. One day the Snipeville stage brought a note. It was for Frankie La Flamme. The handwriting thrilled him. It was evening before he opened it. It was short, a few lines. His eyes filled with tears; he read:

"Jenny Sauvé has died of fever to-day. Your mother is very low. Lose no time.
"MILLY DE LA ROSA."

Music consoles in sorrow. He whistled. Cagy, who knew the contents of the note, informed Weeks. It brought a sad scene to his memory. Brushing his tears aside with the sleeve of his coat, he ordered a buggy, and bade Frankie to get to his mother "as fast as Nelly could put." He but hinted at La

Flamme's intention. The spirited beast threw up her head, pawed vigorously, sniffed the night air, and started.

The road for a few miles was straight and broad; then it curved, followed the river a few miles, became narrow and crooked entering the woods. The night, calm at first, became fretful and broken. Rain changed to sleet, and the wind became cold and pointed. The moon lay amid dark clouds, sending now and then a flickering glance to make darker the harsh river. La Flamme was sure of his road until he entered the forest. Here doubts arose. So many roads branched, some broader and more travelled than the one he was on. He lighted his lamp, fixed it to his dash-board, uttered a prayer for Jenny, and took the road that seemed most travelled. After an hour's drive it led to a deserted logging-camp. Baffled and cold, he turned his horse to seek his first road. The wind was rising. The branches of the trees clashed above his head, thunder seemed human in its mighty groan, pines whistled, lightning played before his eyes, now cracking a branch, now heavily crushing a stately tree. The sleet became more worrying. At first it brought the blood to his cheeks, now it seemed to lay open his face with the keenness of a razor-blade. Stories of ghosts peopled his mind.

A rustle amid the branches, a quick, snappy yell, told him that the dreaded loup-garou was on his track. He pulled his fur coat closer to his shivering body, pressed the musk-rat cap closer to his head, and shouted to his faithful horse. She knew and loved his voice. Her trot became faster, but jerkier. He was on his old road. His lamp tossed and flickered. Sleet blinded him, cold crept through his buckskin gloves, making the reins fall from his hands. His head became dizzy, his limbs stiff. He tried to shake off this growing numbness—curved his mouth to whistle, clapped his hands to his sides, pounded his feet on the bottom of his buggy. It increased his weakness. Gathering his voice-strength, he shouted to his horse, " To Snipe-ville, Nelly !" A hungry fox, buried in fallen brush, barked.

Compulsory confinement often gives boldness to shy creatures. " To accomplish anything in this world requires sacrifice," came to him in his agony. He bent his head, tried to curve his voice to speech. He listened; no sound came. He thought he saw a light. Was it his lamp? The buggy swayed; he felt a sweet, pressing pain.

Jemmie Barbier sat singing in his cabin, wondering "what the night would turn to." He thought he heard a noise, but, as he said afterwards, "who thinks of noise in a storm." "Worst night I have seen in twenty years," he muttered as he went to the door to take a peep at the elements. "Wind's changed; going down as quick as it came up. I'll make a start for Skinny's." Suddenly he became alarmed at a strange noise and a swinging light at the end of his house. Taking his lantern and gun, he cautiously advanced.

His first words were: "Some poor fellow has gone to his reward to-night. Bless my soul, Jim Weeks' Nelly! She couldn't drag the buggy far in that way. It must have upset within a mile of here." Barbier carefully unhitched the stamping, maddened horse. One of the buggy-wheels, coming in contact with the house, was broken and the axle twisted. This seemed to have restrained the poor animal. Gently leading her to the barn, he wrapped her in an old blanket, wishing that Milly or his wife was home "to wisp her a bit." "She'll be herself again," he said, as he quickly hitched his own horse and started out to seek Nelly's driver. He was old, past the seventies, but his arm was strong and his sight was keen.

The reins in one hand, the lantern in the other, he kept his eyes glancing from one side of the road to the other. About a hundred rods from his house, just ahead of his horse's nose, he saw something black lying. Shouting "Whoa, my pet!" he dismounted and approached the lifeless-looking mass. He shook it, saying: "If ye be earthly, in the name of God speak." There was no answer. Getting on his knees, he turned the body over until his light fell on the face. A sigh burst from the old woodsman. "Frankie La Flamme, you're surely not dead!" Cramping his wagon, he lifted the youth tenderly and laid him across the buggy-seat. Starting his horse, he held the limp body until the door was reached; then carried it to his bed and rubbed it long, using such simple remedies as his cabin gave. He was doubtful of success. Sometimes he thought La Flamme was dead; then he blamed his hearing and continued to rub.

"It's time to go," said Mrs. Barbier to Milly,

"and see what's become of your uncle. I worry about him. We can do nothing more. We stayed with her to the last."

"Skinny died a happy death, auntie. Père Monnier said she made her purgatory in this life," said Milly.

"Yes, dear, she died a very happy death. As for purgatory, a little of it wouldn't do any of us a bit of harm."

"Do dying people, auntie, always talk of their young days? Didn't you hear how Skinny spoke of her mother—her eyes bright as coals, but black, black: her father, his old violin, Sister Marie, her husband, and Frankie, who might have been here?"

"Yes, dear, that's my way of thinking. I kind of believe that God shows us the bright spots in our life before he takes us."

"Well, auntie, then I'll talk of you and Uncle Jemmie when I'm dying."

"There may be more to think of than us, child."

Mrs. Barbier and Milly knelt by the side of the old mattress on which Skinny lay, and prayed. On a little fresh straw, covered with a worn-out spread, lay the once laughing Jenny Sauvé, sweet in death.

"We have all to come to this," said Mrs. Barbier, rising; then, turning to the anxious faces that had hurried from their homes on the first noise of Skinny's death, "Wash and dress her. Milly and I are a little sleepy; besides, Jemmie's old, and helpless about getting his own food. Come, Milly, and don't forget Skinny's present— the picture. I'll keep the violin for Frankie."

They passed out, and in a few minutes were in view of the log cabin. "Uncle was just coming for us, auntie," said Milly: "see old Peggin harnessed before the door."

"It was always his way, child, since I've known him." The door was wide open. They entered. Tucked in the cosey bed lay Frank La Flamme, Jemmie Barbier bending over him, towel in hand. His face wore a triumphant smile.

"I've got him where I wanted him. I've got him. Your old man is no slouch, Selina. I've cured him myself. He was dead all morning. About half an hour ago he commenced to live, and is doing first rate since. He's his father, every inch of him; cordy as a beech."

"Since he sleeps, uncle," said Milly, "tell us how and where you found him."

"You little rascal! you're not a bit sleepy."

"Why don't you answer my question, uncle?"

"Because I'm no hand at story-telling. You get him well, and then you'll have the water at first dip."

A few weeks later Frankie lay by the window, gazing at the long, dark line of bleak pines. He had just been told of his mother's death. It was a sad day. Milly had twitted him for promising to write daily, and then "shamefully breaking his promise." Explanations made things worse. She had nursed him back to health; "but," and her eyes showered fire-sparks, "they could only be friends." She had almost said the terrible yes to another. Frankie, left to himself, drew his pocket-pistol charged with sacrifice. It shot the spectre of his mother. Love laughed at its bullets. No other would have the choice of his life; saved from death was to him preserved for a better life. Like most woodsmen, his beliefs were positive. What better life than to be mated with Milly? He pressed his head to the pillow, shut his eyes, and went through the drama "Love." Milly's tip-toeing called him to his surroundings. Love is all ears, ever ready to catch the slightest sound of the object loved. He nestled in his cot, pretending sleep. but letting his half-shut eyes take in the vision.

Woman's eyes are quick; she smiled at his trickery. "Frankie La Flamme, don't you close your eyes when you sleep?" she said. He smiled and was captured. "Guess who's here?" she said. He was indifferent. "Oh, do guess!" she continued. "I'll give the first letter of the name." He shut his eyes. The name of his rival crossed his mind and soured his thoughts. "Guess quick; they come!" she cried. He turned to look her full in the face. Fortune was on the turn: Billy Buttons and Cagy entered the room, Buttons carrying a huge bag. Stepping in front of the sick man's cot, he emptied the bag before him, shouting, "Cagy, make the darned thing clear." Envelopes, big and small, crushed and bulgy, envelopes of all colors and makes, made the strange-looking pile. What a heap of fond dreams! Frankie's eyes were lost in them.

"Sit down, Milly; you have something to hear," said Cagy. "I'm to blame for this whole mess. I told Bill to put in a receiver. Bill was always obliging. To help folks in it went; but in putting it in devil a hole he left to take out the letters. Well, it might have run on till Gabriel blows his trumpet had not La Jeunesse thrown little Brie against it, and smashed the darned thing. The minute it fell, pop came the letters by the bushel. They were all for you in two handwritings. 'Faith,' says I, 'Milly will have reading for six weeks, constant go. Says Whistler, 'She has got the grip on Buttons. She can send him to the jail for obstructing the going of Uncle Sam's mail.' It's a life job at that. Weeks thought it was best to lay the outs and ins of the case before Père Monnier. Whistler said that the père would know all the law in the case, and he advised Billy to take his medicine like a man. Buttons don't fear the face of clay, and he done too much for you when old Jenks' brain cracked for you to bring action against him for a few letters. Père Monnier fixed the thing in a jiffy. He told Buttons to bring you the letters, and hoped the reading would do you and Frankie much good. I hope so. That's all there is to the story, if I was to die on the spot! Of course if you want to be mean—but I don't think there's a drop of that kind in you—you'll report us. I don't care for myself, but Buttons has a lot of mouths to fill."

Tears trickled down the girl's cheeks. "Report you!" she sobbed. "How could you say that of your little girl, Cagy? And you stand there and let him, Billy!"

She was caught in the arms of two old guides who stammered out apologies, Cagy's voice highest, saying, "Milly, didn't I provise there's not a drop of that kind in you, and ain't it so?"

"Milly," said Buttons, "Cagy would knock the man down that would say anything about you. You're a credit to Squidville. If poor Dory was alive, wouldn't she be proud of you! No wonder Jemmie, ay, and for that matter Frankie's daft about you. Cagy, come and let the two youngsters read the pile and have a bit of a talk over it. I'll have no new wrinkles in my business again. Every man must come up to the counter and do his business open; no more receivers for gentle folk in Squidville."

"Don't be rubbing the healing skin on the old sore," said Cagy. "It's all over. Let us go to the kitchen and have a smoke with Jemmie."

"Dinner's all ready," said Selina, poking her head into the room. "It's a cure for sore eyes to see Blind Cagy and Billy Buttons in our house. Yous won't put a foot out of this door to-night. It's little enough that the Snipeville stage can take one day in the year." Cagy was of the same way of thinking; he held the reins.

When he arrived a day late in Squidville his only remark was, "Another man would have remained a couple of days." On this Whistler said, "It seems strange there could be such a storm in Snipeville and not strike us."

A year after Professor Corkey Slithers addressed his pupils: "I have this jocund day received an invitation to the wedding of two of my former pupils, Frankie La Flamme and Milly De La Rosa. Tell your mothers to send flowers to the church next Tuesday, where your teacher and you, my boys and girls, will put up the finest decoration that Squidville shall ever see, if she shall prolong her existence to the end of the world."

"Big-hearted Slithers!" said Weeks. "Knows when to give up," said Buttons. "A gentleman and a scholar," was the common word. Père Monnier heartily laughed. Squidville was happy.

CHAPTER VI.

SKINNY BENOIT'S SON.

"HAVE you heard of Squidville, on the Salmon River? Of course you must. It was there that Bob Stevens fought his famous fight with the big Indian Jock.

"The little stage over yonder at Ransom's runs through Squidville and stops at Porcupine Creek. You say you want fishing; if you do, youngster, that's the place."

The speaker was a tall, angular man with high forehead, indented cheeks, and gray, piercing eyes. He was still lithe and active, although past the forties. It was easy to see that he was a French-Canadian, and his tanned cheeks and shoulder-droop made the guessing of his occupation an easy task. A few days before the rain had come down in torrents, the river was swollen, and thousands of logs, like bits of kindling-wood, were carried down its angry current from Squidville and Porcupine Creek. The rain had ceased, the river subsided, and the choppers had come down to Malone to have their logs measured, and to receive pay for their winter's work. One of them was the speaker, Frank La Flamme; and the man that he wished to visit his mountain home was a clerk of the company that had bought his logs. The clerk promised that his first vacation would be passed in Squidville; and as the stageman was hitching his horses La Flamme, with a "Mind your promise, youngster," hurried off and mounted the stage. An elderly lady, with a noticeable tinge of Sioux blood in her veins, was just then being politely helped into the stage by a grave, dignified, bald-headed merchant, while his business partner was barely able to place by her side a huge basket of groceries. "*Comment ça va*, grandmother. You're early getting ready for the dance." The old lady smiled, muttered "*Oui*," and settled herself to sleep. The bald-headed man, hearing La Flamme's voice, seemed glad. His face, at least, showed some lighter shades akin to laughter.

"Hello, Frank! ain't you comin' in?"

"I guess not, Mr. Ransom."

"Well, Frank, you may do as you please. You promised to pay us the interest, at least, as soon as you sold your logs. If you break your promise I cannot keep mine."

"Mr. Ransom," said La Flamme, holding down his head, "do give me a little time. Times are bad; the new standard has destroyed us this year; and, as if that was not enough, I had to lose my horse with a spavin. What was I to do? I had to go in debt for another, so that I could skid my logs in time. You can wait. You know I'm as honest as the sun. Didn't I deal with you for twenty years, and didn't you always get your pay some time?"

"I won't wait, Frank," was the gruff answer of Mr. Ransom as he politely bowed to his now nodding customer, Grandmother Croquet. It was not Croquet's way to notice what she disdainfully called "Yankee business touches."

"Ransom, you're a scoundrel; you told me to come and trade, and pay when I got ready; now, because I am deep in your books, you throw away the glove and show your hand. I can't pay; so do your best," was La Flamme's rejoinder, hissed through his teeth, while his dark gray eyes became feline in their expression.

The crack of the stageman's whip was the

full-stop mark to the conversation. The old lady woke, rubbed her eyes, and noting La Flamme's sulk, that had spread over his face, muttered, "*Devra avoir hônte*, François"; then gave a sharp look at her basket, shut her eyes, and went asleep. A half-dozen of choppers, with their bright red stockings drawn tightly over their pants' legs, and their wide-rimmed hats set back on their heads, boarded the stage, talking loudly their *patois*, gesticulating, laughing immoderately, presenting to the casual observer that peculiar phase of the French-Canadian character—present contentment.

"Gee up!" said the stageman.

"Get a gait on your horses," said one of the choppers. "I like that horse on the nigh, but his mate's a dandy," said another. "They are breeched and spavined," said a third. "I wouldn't give a dollar mortgage on them," said the fourth, pulling from his inside pocket a huge black bottle of Canadian high-wines. The bottle was carelessly passed around; even the elderly lady with the tinge of Sioux awoke in time to take what Berry, the driver, called "a 'sky-flier' of a pull." La Flamme, with sullen look, held himself aloof from this growing weakness of the French-Canadian who has made the States his home.

It was strange — so strange to his fellow-choppers that little Piquet vowed that "Frank was coming to be an angel."

"There's as much fear of that as a woodchuck leaving his hole when you are around," said big La Jeunesse, looking serious.

"Hand him that bottle, Brie, and let him have an old-time swig; it's the genuine thing. See how it opened Grandmother Croquet's eyes," cried Berry, turning on his seat to see if Andrieux, who hugged the bottle to his chest, would fulfil his commands.

"Andrieux," said La Flamme, drawing his thin lips in the way of his teeth, "I will not touch that cursed stuff. It has been my ruin for many a day. Can't you fellows have fun enough without me? I have bother enough. That miserable beggar the horse-dealer met me an hour ago and made me pay in full for that old horse that he 'palmed' on me as a young beast—yes, all the money that I had, even the interest due to Ransom. I guess it's always the way: if you're poor everybody wants to bite you."

"How much did you give him?" said Berry, cracking his whip.

"One hundred and twenty-five," was La Flamme's doleful reply.

"Heavens!" said Piquet.

"You were taken in," said Andrieux.

"The horse ain't worth fifty dollars. The moment I saw him I told you that he was spavined. Didn't I, Frank?" shouted Brie.

"You fellows know everything about a horse when somebody tells you. Why don't you air your wisdom before a fellow as poor as I be makes a trade?" was La Flamme's sarcastic reply.

"Well, La Flamme"—and Brie pulled from his pocket a huge plug of newly bought tobacco, carefully rolled in a deer-skin bag—"because you have the name of being a kind of horse-jockey; and no matter how good a hand a man might be around horses, he's not such a fool as to give pointers to a jockey."

The discussion came to an abrupt end by Berry jumping from his wagon, dancing and slapping his hands against the side of his big coat, shouting, "Squidville! All out for Squidville!"

Squidville—its origin is lost in obscurity, like

that of most mountain towns in these regions. Billy Buttons, the guide, avows that it is named after a man named Squid, while Blind Cagy says that its name is Skidville, or the place where they skidded logs. The traveller has no escape between these rural historians, whose arguments pro and con are the nightly fascination of Squidville Hotel. Squidville—I prefer the spelling of Buttons—" is the easiest town in the state to find your way in"; that is the first salutation of Jim Weeks, the jolly, fat proprietor of the Hunter's Paradise. The town skulks along the Salmon River for a distance of half a mile. " The number of log cabins in this our city," says Buttons, " is two-and-twenty, sir."

" Mind, we are not counting the hotel, which be a frame house, sir, with nigh twenty beds as fine as silk," Cagy drops in to remark.

There is but one street in this village—Pleasant View. Country folk have their ideas of beauty as well as their city brethren. When Squidville was laid out by Mr. Potter, the genial Weeks—standing on the top of the brae that leads through the woods to Porcupine Creek, and looking at the Salmon River winding itself like a silver thread through the bits of green wood and marshy meadow-land, as if inspired, so says Cagy — cried out: "Boys, a pleasant view!" That exclamation named Squidville's only street, and immortalized the name of Weeks. The last house on Pleasant View looks like a cross between a Queen-Anne cottage and a lumbering shanty. There is a liberty-pole before the door, and a tattered flag flying from it. Swinging from a post, ornamented in lines of red and white, plainly telling of Weeks' love for his old trade, is a flaming golden sign:

"Hunter's Paradise.
Jim Weeks, Prop.
Best Summer Resort in the Adirondacks."

Before the door, shivering in the cold, ran two bow-legged, long-eared hounds, whining and waving their tails. Grandmother Croquet, fiercely holding her basket, was the first to amble from the stage. Weeks, bareheaded and bowing, escorted her to the hotel, while Buttons remarked that he did not know where Croquet got the money to buy such a lot of things, and Cagy, hot with rage, avowed that Croquet's folks "have as good a right to money as any folks in this darned country." Mrs. Croquet and her basket safe in the care of Weeks, the wood-choppers sprang lightly from the stage and were soon busy helping the slow Berry to unhitch and feed his curdy-looking team. Kindness is a mountain virtue; it is the golden link that unites these poor people and makes life pleasant during the long, sullen stretches of the winter months. There are scores of men and women daily met with, up and down the road of life, who have a kind of philosophy that tells them that every natural event in their lives is heralded by a supernatural one. The poet was in sight of this when he wrote, " Coming events cast their shadows before." It is useless to argue with such people in the vain effort of converting them. Would it not be pleasant to be able to write of this superstition as a corn only found on the toes of the ignorant? Very; but would it be true? If biography be not a grand conspiracy against truth, as some one said of history, many prominent agnostics wore a tight-fitting shoe.

La Flamme was the last to jump from the stage, and when he had done so he leaned against the stage-shafts as if dazed. His ordinary habit would have been to lend Berry a willing hand to unyoke his team. Brie, noticing this, shouted, " La Flamme, are you dreaming?"

Yes, he was dreaming.

A few days before a blackbird, during a heavy snow-storm, had beaten its way through the paper pane and sought safety and rest on the shoulder of his wife, as she busied herself preparing the brown johnny-cake and the thick, black coffee for her husband. La Flamme in the natural goodness of his heart, instead of killing the drooping bird and averting ill luck, caught it, gave it something to eat, tenderly nursed it, and when the storm was spent restored it to liberty and its native haunts. Dreaming there by the stage-shaft, this bird once more crossed his vision. We are but the sport of thought. His Canadian mother had often sung to him what a dire messenger of ill luck was the blackbird. Her teaching had not been lost. The kindliness of the man's heart had saved the bird, but in that very act he saw the beginning of his misfortune. Why did the horse-dealer, who lived in Belmont, happen to be in Malone? Why did Ransom, in whose store he had traded for twenty years, threaten him with law? He could not answer these questions a few minutes ago; now it was easy to do so when the scene in his cabin a few days ago came to his memory. It was his failure to kill the blackbird, and black superstition drove kindness from the wood-chopper's warm heart. "Why didn't I kill that cursed bird?" he muttered. "Misfortune is on me and mine." How often has an accident, taking place at the right moment, confirmed as a lifelong truth the silliest superstition! It was to be so with Frank La Flamme.

Brie led one horse to the stable, Berry another. As they did so the stage-shafts fell to the ground.

The dreamer woke and walked over to Weeks, the two dogs executing a kind of dance around him. It was at this moment that Buttons, sitting on an empty soap-box on the piazza, remarked to Cagy "that it was the first time in his life that he had seen Frank slow to make of his dogs."

"And look at them," says Cagy, "with their front paws on his vest, as if they were Christians."

La Flamme took no notice of his dogs, but, bidding *bon voyage* to Andrieux, mounted the piazza. Buttons had a dozen questions ready for him, when Cagy, with a knowing nudge, brought Buttons' ear close to his mouth and whispered: "La Flamme's little girl is in the store, crying."

"You don't say so!" was Buttons' reply as he and Cagy craned their necks—striking an attitude peculiar to an Adirondack guide.

"Is pa here, Mr. Weeks?" said the dark-eyed, scantily clad little maid, looking piteously in the landlord's face.

"Yes, dear, he has just put his foot on the piazza. And what's the matter with my girl to-day? You have been crying," said the landlord, rubbing away the child's tears with the back of his big hand.

"Because mamma is sick, very sick. The priest and doctor are with her, and she wants my papa," sobbed the child.

La Flamme stood in the doorway; the words smote his heavy heart. "Aily! Aily!" he cried.

"Papa—mamma!" sobbed the child, as she fell in her father's arms.

About a quarter of a mile from the village hostelry, in one of the two-and-twenty low, shambling log houses, lived La Flamme. His house was built in Squidville's only style—logs mortised together, with here and there a huge iron clamp, "to steady her a bit," as Cagy used to remark. The space between the logs was filled up with rough mortar. The effect of such a house on the eye was far from pleasing; yet in point of comfort it far excelled the ordinary country frame house. It was one of Buttons' ordinary remarks that "such houses were native to the soil," and there was much truth in this observation.

When dark clouds teem on the mountain's brow, and fierce winds drive the sleet over the lowlands, making it as prickly as sharp-pointed needles, there is an indescribable comfort in a log cabin, with its laughing fire of crackling pine logs. A stranger would easily guess that there was something wrong in this cabin from the continual opening and shutting of the door, and the dozen or more women, with black shawls closely drawn about their heads, that formed themselves in little knots before the door, talking in a subdued voice. One of them, a woman of coarse features and rugged build, leaving the others, pulled the latch-string and entered.

"Glad to see you, Mrs. Poulet," said Buttons, who had led the village in its race to the sick-house.

"Will she be at herself again?" inquired Cagy.

Throwing her head back, and letting the shawl fall on her broad shoulders, Mrs. Poulet scornfully rejoined, "You fellows here, drinking up all the air that the poor woman should have;" and then with stately step advanced to the sick woman's bed.

"That's a tomboy for you!" was the only remark that slipped the tongue of the crestfallen Cagy.

"Poor Milly!" said Mrs. Poulet, bending over the sick woman; then, turning to La Flamme, who was kneeling by the bedside of his wife, pillowing her drooping head on his tawny arm: "Better send Aily to some of the neighbors. She is breaking her heart, poor thing."

Aily was leaning over her mother's face kissing the damp sweat from her forehead. La Flamme did not hear: his eyes were fastened on a rough print representing Christ as the good pastor—bought years ago from a Jewish pedlar, and pinned to the side wall near his bed.

"She is getting worse," said Mrs. Poulet, turning away her head to hide her tears.

At this remark the young priest, who had stood by the foot of the bed, now knelt by the side of it and commenced to pray aloud in French. He was joined by a dozen voices; even those out-of-doors knelt on the cold, damp ground to utter, in response to the rich, bass voice of their priest, a prayer for Milly La Flamme. The doctor, a thin, talkative man, whose hero was Thomas Paine, removed his fur cap. This doctor used to take my place when the roads between Snipeville and Squidville were blocked. It is told to this day in Squidville that his lips moved as if in prayer.

"I think it would ease her to have warm bottles to her feet," said Mrs. Croquet, panting from her quick walk.

"You can have all the bottles you want in my store," said Weeks.

"I'll have them in a jiffy," said Buttons, opening the door.

"It's useless," said the doctor.

"Ay, useless sure," muttered Mrs. Poulet.

La Flamme's wife looked at her husband; his eyes were still fastened on the print; then her eyes wandered to it. Aily, wondering, looked at her parents' faces and set hers in the same direction.

"*Bon Pasteur*," said La Flamme.

"*Aidez ma mère*," responded Aily.

"She is dead," said the doctor.

"Dead," repeated the priest.

"She was a good woman," said Mrs. Croquet.

"Good and bad all together must go," said Mrs. Poulet, pulling the shawl over her head.

"It's a hard one for poor Frank," ejaculated Weeks, with tears running down his cheeks.

"She died like an angel," said Brie.

"She went off in the crack of a whip," said Berry.

"Here's the bottles," said Buttons, opening the door.

"Yer too late, Buttons; and she don't want bottles on the other side. God rest her," said Cagy.

"Amen," replied Buttons. "But you don't tell me it's all over with her?"

"She's as dead as a nail," said Cagy, with a long-drawn sigh.

"Ay, sure, Billy Buttons," put in a dozen voices, "Milly La Flamme is dead."

Squidville has a graveyard on the Porcupine road, a good half-mile from the village. It is a bit of clearing of about three acres in the heart of the woods, fenced in with huge burnt logs. In the centre stands a rough wooden cross, and here and there a black pine stump, looking like sentinels of the dead. To this quiet spot came the body of Milly La Flamme, borne on a rough country wagon, drawn by Weeks' pair of four-year-old bay colts, followed by Berry and the Squidville stage, carrying La Flamme, the weeping Aily, and their relatives.

Behind the stage came the people of Squidville mounted on all kinds of rigs.

The last prayer said, and the first shovelful of clay thrown on the coffin by Père Monnier, La Flamme led his little girl from her mother's grave. Before he had reached the stage a hand was lightly laid on his shoulder.

He turned around. "Good-day, Frank." "Good-day, Sheriff Matson." "I am sorry for your troubles, Frank," continued the sheriff, "and had I known of them I would not be here to-day. Poor fellow! you have trouble enough without me bothering you, but" — and the sheriff's voice was troubled—"have courage, Frank. I will go home."

"Sheriff, I know it is not your fault to be here to-day. You must do your duty. You come from Ransom. Well, there's no use in putting you to a second trip. All I have is the two horses and wagon that La Jeunesse is driving. Take them; they will pay the debt. There's no luck for me in this place. Tell Ransom, sheriff, that it's the old story: get on a storekeeper's books and slavery begins. That was Milly's constant warning, sheriff; she often used to say, 'It is better, Frank, to do without something than go in debt for it.' But Milly is dead, dead! sheriff, and my motherless child and I, as soon as we say good-by to Père Monnier, will start for the West. Some day Aily and I might have money enough to buy Milly a headstone."

"Go away, papa, and leave mamma here?" said the child.

"No, mamma is in heaven. Aily; and heaven is in the West as well as here."

CHAPTER VII.

THE RETURN OF CORKEY SLITHERS.

It was a saying in Squidville, "Live in it once, and you'll live in it again." I am free to confess there is something in the saying.

Professor Slithers left us vowing vengeance, shaking, as he put it, "the pulverized dust-particles from his feet forever." After two years of wandering, no one knows where, he returned, which, in Squidville at least, made the saying authentic.

It is of his coming, and the strange things that thereafter happened, I write—rather copy from my old yellow diary. And, by the way, to quote friend Buttons, "the past is a mighty queer customer." What memories this old faded copy-book brings—memories of other days, when I was a younger man, full of life, finding merriment in these mountains and dear companionship with brave mountaineers! "Times change as change they must," is an old refrain that comes with a saddening influence as I write.

I notice my hair, once so black and curly, is white, and my face as wrinkled as Skinny Benoit's. The place is changed—or is it that my change changes all things? I wonder which it is.

A truce, old memories! you blind my eyes! you keep from my sight these pencilled pages, that tell of the return of Professor Slithers.

It is a habit of mine to pencil, from day to day, the things that give laughter-food in Squidville town. Fun, honest fun, does not care a rap with whom it keeps company, tickling poor and rich alike, oftener, methinks, in company with the poor man. What light it brings to his life, what joy to his poor household, authors, in various ages, have attested. It has lit his gloom, swept away his sorrow, cured many a pain and ache better than the doctor.

It is a theory of mine that no dyspeptic can make a good physician. I have put many on the road to recovery by telling a good story.

I remember how James Duquette showed signs of betterment after hearing of Slithers' antics. Maybe some others would like to hear them. That's my only excuse for copying. "Maybe," I say, but I know not.

I was, as is my usual custom, sitting in Weeks'

hotel one evening, just as the stage-coach rattled to the door, when to my astonishment who pops off but Slithers in a brand-new suit of black, crowned with an elegant high hat. His gloves were surely kid, while in one hand he carelessly dallied a gold-headed cane. He had baggage. I believe it was this fact that gathered the crowd. I could hear Buttons distinctly say, "Slithers is on the ups," while Blind Cagy was poking fun at the stay-at-home boys, and jocularly pointing to the big trunk, on which was written, in large white letters,

"PROFESSOR SLITHERS. MEDIUM.
T. O. S."

These last letters were full of worry to the crowd. Buttons, who had, as he said, "a long experience in tackling all kinds of lettering, straight, crooked, and slanting," had to shake his head and admit that "a-ciphering out T. O. S. was too much for a common skull like his," all of which added to the puzzle, and stimulated wonder. The professor was not unmindful of this as he stepped on the hotel piazza, shaking the landlord's hand warmly, and saluting him in a high-pitched strain, after this way: "Weeks, my bucolic old friend, *facile princeps* among the stomach-ticklers of the Adirondacks, a thing of beauty, a joy to see — yes, Weeks, behold your peripatetic Slithers, now a comforter of humanity by occultism — yes, Slithers, T. O. S." Emphasis dwelling long on these letters, aided by a rolling of his eyes, deeper still made the mystery.

"There be something unnatural," said Sal Purdy, "in these same letters; they're not mortal." The trunk was soon out of sight, stored in a room, and the curiosity-crowd went its way, having a new nut to crack.

Squidville was in need of gossip, and the strange letters came as a shower after a long drouth, or as a thaw after a long frost-spell. Tongues were loosened and discussion became a pleasure. I was appealed to, as a man of learning, to solve a mystery that had been called the "dark secret" by the genial Père Monnier. I but added to the puzzle.

Slithers was not unmindful of public excitement; it was an excellent advertisement, and he utilized it in a way which, to use one of our phrases, "hurried the grist to his mill."

Hiring the school-house, he billed the town, discarding the old-fashioned way of "making announcers by bell-ringing." These bills showed the cunning of the professor, and read:

"T. O. S.

SLITHERS!

THE ONLY SLITHERS

MEDIUMISTIC OCCULTIC SLITHERS!

—:UNRIVALLED SLITHERS!:—

PSYCHOLOGICAL SLITHERS!

☞ *One and All Invited!* ☜

Price, 10 *cents.*

N. B.—Rapping Phenomena Later.

. T. O. S."

The school-house was unable to contain all those who were drawn in the hope that the mystic letters might be expounded. Slithers was not to be so easily caught. As he used to say in former years, " He was a man that never threw away a good thing." A taking advertisement is not to be despised. The lecture was on " Planchette, the Despair of Science," and was as mystic to his hearers as were the letters. I quote Cagy's criticism, which, if not as elegant as that of the professional reviewer's, was more to the point:

"You might as well follow a loon in the water as Slithers, or a fox on foot. He may understand himself, but if he does he'll soon stew out his skull."

It is an opinion of mine that the more mystic is humbuggery the more certain will it be to succeed. Although in public we laugh at the bogies of our children, to please society, yet in private we are children hushed to sleep with the same bogies. Slithers, give him his due, knew the animal man, and gave him the desired medicine.

It had its contemplated effect, which was to draw the crowd.

Seeing things go his way, he hired a house, hung out his sign, and boldly proclaimed that he would give nightly seances wherein "rapping, table-tipping phenomena, virtual manifestations, grandmother testimony, future-laid-bare, and similar occurrences of the most momentous and startling nature would be produced by the magic wand of

"Yours truly,

"CORKEY SLITHERS, T. O. S."

This sign was noticed in a long editorial article in the *Porcupine Pioneer*, whose editor,

Joel Spratt, was a Methodist deacon and a bitter foe of Spiritualism. With this editorial Slithers' fame swept the adjacent towns, bringing him investigators and their dollars—that were more to his taste. Joel, in his sledge-hammer way, contended that if " a mortal wayfarer was to cast off the slough and put on immortality, setting out straight forward for mansions of eternal perpetuity and bliss, he would neither want to come to the mortal, nor, no matter how closely he might hug that same fool-idea, he couldn't get here, for no angel would let him pass." "If," continued the editorial, " the same fellow went off into eternal perdition, or in other words to Sheol, he would have to stay there and make the most of it. Men might be bribed, but Satan—never."

This last word was in large capitals, and was, in the *Porcupine* office, supposed to be the clinch " to the powerfullest bit of writing that Joel ever greased paper with."

Slithers, confident of his attraction, called the editorial " buggy," and thus, by the dexterous use of a well-known word, took the wind from Joel's sails. He even went further, and invited the sceptic deacon to " come and eat his words in the presence of ocular demonstration."

Squidville loved dearly a row, and, seeing a chance lost through the deacon's cowardice, was not slow to applaud the professor, a sure way of making the deacon feel its grievance.

So things went, adding fame and money to Slithers. But he was ambitious, and, like many another, to ambition he succumbed.

Not content with worsting the *Porcupine*, he challenged me to give testimony to "the truth of his manifestations." It will be said of me, I trust, that I covet no man's back seat. Besides, in those days, I was as ready for a fray as any man in the mountains.

I had, if I write it myself, and without egotism, an ordinary amount of strong common-sense always at my disposal.

Now to let Corkey know that I was hostile to him would have been doubly arming him, and no adversary is entitled to more than is his due, so I wrote over my signature a card to the *Pioneer*, with Joel's warm connivance, fathering the theories of Mr. Corkey, and demanding that he may not be condemned until his case was, as we put it, "sat upon."

This was a "pleasant surrender," said the professor, who was not slow to send me, hastily, the following note:

"*Hunter's Paradise,*
"Wednesday.

"DEAR DOCTOR:
"*Quid pro quo.* You are respectfully invited to my seance to-night, which begins at nine, and is under the control of Benjamin Franklin.

> 'Sweet voices will speak to thee
> From out the other shore—
> Sweet voices will speak to thee
> And tell of days of yore.'
>
> "CORKEY SLITHERS, T. O. S."

I persuaded a few friends to join me, among them, by hard work, Joel Spratt. Jim Weeks, as he always is, was willing to go where a bit of fun might be started. As the night was cold, I had an opportunity to wear my big buffalo-coat, whose pockets were, as well befits a country doctor's, capacious. Keeping my own mind, I slipped into one of them what I had long planned should be used to test Corkey's marvels.

We quietly sauntered down the street, calling at the post-office to take Buttons, whose laughing fellowship was much in a crowd.

The professor was located in one of the ordinary log houses.

He had, with an eye to business, decorated the homely abode with bunting, nailed a flag with the mystic T. O. S. to the chimney, while bills hanging from the door told of him as "the bright particular star in the firmament of occultic wisdom, the Stanley in the field of psychology."

Corkey was there to meet and invite us "to the most rigorous investigation, in order that we should return to our homes with our preconceived vulgar notions and deceits fully eradicated." "You are free, gentlemen," he continued. "In fact, I invite the most thorough scientific researches. Scoffers," casting a withering eye on Spratt, "shall pensively return to their homes to-night, muttering, as they go, the imperishable thought of William Shakespeare, 'What fools we mortals be!'"

The inside was tastefully decorated, for our parts, with pictures that the professor claimed were the work of the spirits, who, in their leisure moments, had given their time to ornament the chapel of their votary.

The house was divided into two apartments: one for receiving visitors, containing chairs, a table strewn with correspondence, a writing-desk, where the professor, wheeling in his chair, transacted, as he termed it, "his multifarious business." His desk was ornamented by a bust of

Benjamin Franklin, the presiding deity of the place.

Corkey was on the most intimate terms with the philosopher, as was evidenced by his addressing him: "Benny, say out your say, old boy," or, "Governor, do your duty." Let it be written, also, that the professor had no fear in the presence of the mightiest of our race. Alexander the Great, Hannibal, Pompey, Napoleon, Wellington, and Grant came at his sweet will and conversed on the most trivial things, in the most peculiar way. On one occasion the victor of Waterloo was known to give valuable hints on hop-raising. It is needless to say that Wellington became a general favorite, from his kindly interest in the people of Squidville.

It was, as Slithers well put it, "a wonderful change in spirit-land that made a warrior bold and brave become a man of peace and betake himself to the study of hops." That he had made no ordinary progress, was well shown by his practical hints about manuring the vines, cultivating between the rows, and spraying them often.

The other room was small, and was used for sittings. The little window that lit it was boarded up in such a way that not a glimmer of light was possible. In this room was a plain deal table about twelve feet long, and known as the "seance-table." Rough, backless seats ran along this table for the investigators who were satisfied with rapping, table-tapping, and, to use the language of the professor, "kindred phenomena."

In this room "ponderable bodies without appreciable agency in the presence of Corkey Slithers were to be moved." For the more sceptical there was a cabinet in one corner, where material manifestations were given, where the "disembodied spirits put on the corporeal for better identification, and came to breathe to their living dear ones messages of hope and guarantees of immortality." Another article in this room, that played an important part, was an automaton music-box.

Corkey held that "spirits were extremely susceptible to music, that they took to it as a duck to water, that it was in fact their element." Declaring himself "the concatenation of mediumistic powers," being a musical, writing, speaking, drawing, and healing medium, he was duly qualified to make this announcement.

The entrance-fee to this mystic shrine was the sum of one dollar, prepaid, the rest of the house "being free at a quarter prepaid."

"Let us go the apple-core at once, Slithers," said Buttons, handing him a dollar, followed by our party with an alacrity that brought a sparkle to his eyes.

"That is true student-form," said the professor. "It is readily seen you are the type of investigators welcomed by every teacher of occultic science who yearns to conquer an empire for his new art. Gentlemen, be seated within. The benches will accommodate your party very easily. I do not apologize for the poor furniture, as spirits, free, untrammelled from flesh-desires, no longer hunger for the flesh-pots of Egypt. I believe the deacon may accuse me of being biblical. I am proud to own that that book is at my fingers' ends, as is most books." Here he coughed, and waited for our praise. Seeing that his bait was not a lure, he continued:

"Gentlemen, to business. Honest investigators, in the name of Benjamin Franklin I bid you welcome, and shall give every opportunity that honesty can ask for a free and full investigation. Gentlemen, there are conditions for a seance that the medium must demand. Electricity requires wires to give the distant message, seed darkness to germinate, sunlight to grow.

Nature has her conditions, and only when these are fulfilled does she deign to unfold herself. Am I distinctly and pertinently understood?" Noting that no one rose to offer comment, he continued:

"Darkness is a necessary condition for physical manifestations, and I assume and insist upon that condition. That is all. You are free, before the seance, to poke into every hole and corner, that you may satisfy yourself of the genuineness of the seance you are about to witness. Buttons, bring in a lamp. Deacon, leave nothing in this chamber untouched. You hold the negative of my affirmative, and hence it is your duty to know that there can be no room for trickery."

It was at this time that Buttons remarked to me that the nail of the little finger of the professor's right hand was "uncommonly long and pointed." I made a mental registry, and, with a sharp shot of my eyes, verified it. The search of the deacon revealed nothing that might assist in roguery. We were ready, and, joined by a few irritable-looking ladies, sat around the table in utter darkness, hands touching, hearts beating, those of the women being audible, waiting a sign. The spirits were, to use Corkey's words, "unable to make connection" for a long time. It seemed to me hours. During this sitting I had this thought, which afterwards was pencilled in my diary: "Solitary confinement is odious to humanity." To rouse the spirits the professor resorted to his music-box, grinding out "Sweet Marie," and this failing proposed that the company should join in song, leading off with "Nearer, my God, to Thee." This hymn exhausted his supply, but the singing of "Marching Through Georgia" and "Suwanee River" was kept up by the lusty throat of William Buttons.

Finally there was a jerk at the table. With it song ceased and a dead silence pervaded the room. This silence was broken by the low moan of one of the ladies, who swayed to and fro, giving a motion to the table, and exciting her companion to such a state that she saw stars dancing over my head, and heard voices giving messages. Her excitement and utterances had a nervous effect on the deacon, who began to sway and mutter. I was as cool as a cucumber, while Buttons, who sat by my right, and whose hands touched mine, was equally cool, claiming that the stars "couldn't be over my skull, or his eyes would twig them in a jiffy."

Soon there was a faint rapping—rather scratching—on the table. "If you are a spirit give three raps," said the professor, who had left the table. The raps came. "Who are you? Let me run over the alphabet."

This was done, and Percy Jenkins' name spelled out. We all knew Percy as a big-hearted fellow, who hadn't much here, and we were anxious to hear how he thrived on the other side.

"Ask him, Slithers," said Buttons, "how does he like his new job, or if he is working at all. You know he wasn't much of a hand over here."

He had hardly spoken when one of the ladies yelled, "There he is!—by the side of Deacon Spratt!—circling round and round like a butterfly!"

Sure enough, there he was, staggering even Buttons, who could not but say, "This beats the devil!"

It was then that I carefully drew my syringe from my big pocket, charged as it was with burning chemicals, and watched my opportunity. It was not long in coming. Suddenly a cold hand touched my ear, and a luminous face peered into mine. "Now or never," said I as I squirted the syringe's contents into the vanishing face.

There was a wild, agonized yell, and a falling as if the cabinet was tumbling down.

I jumped from my seat, ran for the lamp, and threw its light on the suspected corner. There, with his hands pressed heavily to his face, screaming with pain, crouched Corkey Slithers in a long, white nightshirt, "decorated," as Buttons said, " for the event."

Piteously he begged for mercy, a little ointment to ease the pain, and a few hours to leave town forever—all of which I readily granted in memory of other days when he was a better man.

" Well, I never thought that of Corkey," said Buttons. " I know now who done the rapping; that nail of his ain't long for nothing."

" Your humbuggery has cost you dearly," said the deacon. " Yes; humbuggery, Corkey ! Yes! you are a man of sin, and I beseech you to repent, for you know not when the hand of the Lord will smite you in His wrath."

" True for you," said Buttons. " This kind of capering can bring no good."

Corkey sobbed like a whipped child, and offered to give up our money.

"Come, boys," said I, "leave him to his own thoughts. And as to the money—you will need it, Corkey, to carry you far away from Squidville—the farther the better."

"Honesty is the best policy," said the deacon as we wended our way home.

Buttons, always fighting for the under dog, in bidding us good-night, said, "Poor, burned Corkey! How will he get to the railway? And if he's around when folks get up they'll murder him. It's only last Sunday I heard Père Monnier say, 'Lend a helping hand to the weak and fallen.' I—I have half a mind to hitch up and take him to safety."

Slithers by the morning had vanished, leaving masks, headgear, crowns of every description, and a brass sign advertising "Corkey Slithers — Teacher of Occultic Science," to pay his board-bill.

CHAPTER VIII.

AN OLD MUSICIAN.

IT was his way, Père Monnier's way, to pay an annual visit to Montreal. As he used to say, "A man should keep in touch with civilization, if it was only for a few days every twelvemonth."

Old Anna, the good priest's housekeeper, thought differently, and was often heard to say, even in his presence, that it was a mad rush for old and half-backed books that took him to the city. If her position was disputed, as it was sure to be, by Napoleon, the man servant, she would tap her old carpet-slipper quickly on the floor, and, turning with a sarcastic twist from his tantalizing words, poke the fire, nodding her head and muttering:

"Books, ay, books! If he hadn't enough of them! Books! You cannot stir for them! Picked up everywhere, poking on his knees in every old store, paying his good money, and carting them here as if they were gold. Books!

Many's the one's head they have put out of kilter."

The père's only response to such tirades from his constant friend was a hearty laugh, the lifting of some old half-clad tome, and shaking it at her. She feared "the black art that slept between the leaves," and a shake was enough to silence one whose policy was, "It's better to be quiet if your noise troubles your betters."

Not a few of Père Monnier's parishioners thought as Anna did, as was shown by the presents they brought their pastor. If they were from home any length of time, they were sure to return with some book or other, fished from a dust-heap in some old book-stall. The more worn and foxed the better it was thought to please the père. They had an idea that books, like wine, grow with age. They grasped a truth. From such a strange way of increasing his library many "queer customers" stood shoulder to shoulder: Byron a helpmate to a stray copy of Jeremy Taylor; the *Summa* of St. Thomas supporting the arch scoffer Voltaire; rollicking Lever in his shirt-sleeves bending over Gury. Each book, strange as his housing, was known to the père, who had a tale of how Le Roy brought this raggy fellow as a New Year's gift, or how Rosalie found that giant bursting with syllogisms modestly sleeping beneath a heap of modern romances and Montreal dust. He was proud of his books, and boasted of the intuitive taste of his parishioners, who so easily discerned, amid lesser lights, the sleeping wizards of the olden time.

Whether for books, or to rub against civilization for a few days, the evidence favoring the former, Père Monnier, leaving his little property in the safe custody of Napoleon and Anna, had gone to Montreal. It was winter-time, to him the most pleasant of the seasons. The land lay white in snow. The bare and bold mountains were covered with the same soft mantle. Trees wove around their nakedness many a fantastic ice design, prettier than their green summer gown. The rivers and ponds were the scenes of skating-tournaments, the music, the merry, laughing voices of the young. On the roads sleigh-bells jingled, while the light and graceful cutters, bowing to each other, gave the occupants a moment of banter.

Holding up a red pocket-handkerchief, by the side of the little coal-box station, as the Montreal train was rounding the curve, the engine slackened pace, and soon, puffing and panting, stopped at the station. Père Monnier, with a bow to the conductor, entered the car, and was soon lost in his Breviary. The scenery along the route, for the most part picturesque, was so well known to him that he preferred to finish his "office" rather than chat with old friends and evoke old memories. Being well known, he had to endure what that entails—a touch on the shoulder, a slight tap on the back, a warm hand-squeeze, and many a hearty *bon jour*. These salutations were always followed by the père's rapid cross-examining as to the health, wealth, gladness, or sorrow of the family, and they not infrequently ended by whispering into the père's ear, " My son Johnny [or, " My daughter Eliza "] has a book as long as my arm, and as thick as my calf, full of gosh queer lettering for M. le Curé." How the cross-examiner's eyes would flash as his mind wandered to his library, and speculated on what shelf could he find room for the latest love-token !

Soon St. Henri was passed, and the père, opening his little grip, put away his Breviary, and was ready when the porter called out, " Montreal—Bonaventura station ! All out ! This way, sir !"

In another moment he was one of a half-running, eager crowd, peering this and that way, some to discover friends, others as if in a moment they could tell what a Canadian city and people were like. Sleighs were ready, and warm furs to wrap, and furry men with red or black toques to persuade, argue, threaten, grab your bag, and if they succeeded in seating you in their sleigh to purr like a cat, mount the dickey, make faces at their beaten rival, singing some familiar Canadian ditty.

But Père Monnier resisted alike persuasion, argument, and threat. He preferred to saunter slowly through the streets. Being a man fond of humankind, and with but few opportunities of contact with human nature of a type different from that to be seen in his own little mountain parish, he enjoyed the sight of the many faces to be met upon the busy thoroughfares and the quiet streets of the great city. It was not only books that he gathered up and took home with him from these periodical visits, but recollections of faces, and characters, and sayings that remained fresh ever after. It was a good hour from the midday meal, and in that time his sauntering would bring him to St. Patrice, where a hearty greeting was sure to await him. He had not gone far when his eyes, so quick when sinners or books were their objects, greeted an old bookstore and curio-shop. It was a find, and, explorer as he was, he would enter and note it on his map. In front of the door were two rickety deal tables, one lacking a foot, and leaning so heavily to the maimed side that the slightest touch gave the onlooker an awkward feeling at the groundward movement of its contents. By the dexterous use of a string, and the keen eye of the bookseller, the falling proved delusive, and many a passer-by was saved an apology. The tables were covered by well-thumbed, badly written stories in rough paper covers, with a few coatless religious works to keep the motley throng in order. The inside corresponded to the outside in pleasing confusion. The store was long and narrow, and every nook was ingeniously utilized. Shelf after shelf crept up the wall, bulging full of worth and trash lovingly hugging each other. It was a strange mingling of brain-children, who spat spleen at each other in life, standing shoulder to shoulder, presenting a stiff line to dust and flies. And what a friendship! When one was taken, how lonely and sad looked his companions, and how quickly they closed ranks! The floor was equally interesting: a huge clock of the seventeenth century, once the possession of a famous French beauty, solemnly ticking time and life away; an armchair, cracked, squeaky, and soiled, whereon the chivalrous Champlain once sat; a sword, good, bright, and trusty, of Maisonneuve; a little silver crucifix of the gallant Brébeuf; a gold medal of Marguerite Bourgeoys; a cane of Montcalm; Montgomery's cap; ancient china, rare dishes, Japanese ware, Indian relics, bits of rare-colored carpets, daggers, pistols, long-barrelled guns, water-colored daubs, engravings, something to catch civilized and savage, a medley of climes and times, history that is mute.

Amidst these sat, or walked, the old bookseller, wise and witty, genial to the lovers of things artistic, a hater of pretensions and superficial book-knowledge. He was of an old school, and would not sell a rare book to a dunce. He read a face as easily as he told the time of his clock. No one was importuned to buy, and every article had its price plainly marked. That price was honest, and no amount of persuasion could change it.

"Talk, sir, has no effect on my prices; they

are honest, sir—a bare living; you see, I have to deal in all things to do it. I guarantee that you shall find your purchase what it was bought for; that is John Thompson's reputation; it was my father's, who kept sixty years in Edinburgh, friend of Wally Scott, sir, who gave him that reputation."

That bit of personal history was a warning to the purchaser to buy at the marked price or to go elsewhere. To the genuine book-lover what hand was warmer, whose eyes were brighter, than those of honest John Thompson? He lies in Mount Royal, sleeping these many years, but how plainly his figure comes to me as I write. I see the lithe and supple frame, bent a bit by age, clad in the loved Scotch tweed "sent from hame by Brother Jed," as he used to say with a long Scotch drawl; the talking, merry blue eyes that told a story quicker than the tongue, and with more art; the domelike skull well thatched by long, glossy white hair, fringing his tam-o'-shanter cap. It was love at first sight between the warm-hearted père and the honest Scotchman.

"Just look around and see if I have not something that you need. I know you want no help. You'll find a step-ladder that will take you to the roof—a little shaky, but safe. A bookman like you, pére, needs no ladder. Christopher North, when climbing like a monkey from one book-shelf to another, used to say to my father:

"'Donald, maun, there's nothing hard to mortals; ay, maun, there's something in that same saying.'"

A breaking of words to win the père's heart.

"I will do so, and I warrant if I want a book I can imitate the monkey-movements of Christopher North," rejoined Père Monnier.

"As I think of it," said the bookseller, "I have a splendid edition of Lactantius, Oxford copy, 1684, best edition. How thoroughly they made books in those days! Those that survive have, as Hazlitt says, 'the pure, silent air of immortality.' Like him, I hate the dust and smoke and noise of modern literature, froth, puffery, skim-milk, waste paper, stuff to light the morning fires with. Yes, sir, but Wally Scott, Bobbie Burns—ay, even Charlie Dickens, that they hoot nowadays as a sentimentalist, will live. They will bury your realists; little Nell cannot be snuffed out by every tasteless brat that dirties paper. But let me show you Lactantius. It once had a place in Sterne's library; strange, is it not? His name is written on the fly-leaf; yes, yes, Laurence Sterne, author of "Tristram Shandy." Who writes a book like that nowadays? Listen to your little men criticising him; they say 'he is bound to die'—nonsense!—star-bombarding. I would not want to see one of those mannikins enter my store. Let him do his prating; there will always be some one to need stove-paper."

The old bookman laughed, and bent over his desk. As he did so a thin, spare figure entered, wrapped tightly in an old brown cloak, carrying a little package carelessly folded in an old newspaper. He swept his large, lustrous almond eyes on every nook of the book-store, and then with a strange, hurrying step and startled face expression, brushed past Père Monnier, and dropped gracefully into the chair of Geoffrey Champlain.

"Here, père," said the bookseller, "is Lactantius; see Sterne's handwriting! Take a seat and examine it. I want to see what I can do for Count Henry. Poor fellow! titles don't amount to much when there is nothing in the pocketbook."

These last words were whispered in the père's ear.

Great as Père Monnier's love was for books,

it was greater for men. He merely glanced at the Lactantius, and used it as a screen to cover his real thought, which was a growing interest in the ill-clad but noble occupant of Champlain's chair.

"*Bon jour*, Count Henry! A raw day for you to be around. I have not sold the book, but will; it's rare."

"That is sad to me," said the count, bending his head, his long, bony fingers playing with the package. By the peculiar emphasis placed on some word and his use of the pronoun, it was easy to tell that he was a foreigner whose book English was better than his colloquial.

"I do so wish it to be sold; my circumstance is so poor, and the Brunetaires will make me to pay my chamber or leave it to-day. It is so sad to me," and tears, little glassy globules, pin-points, came to the corner of his eyes, ran into a furrow, waited for comrades, and then, embracing, sped down his cheek.

"There is much douleur in life, Mr. Thompson, but—" and with an innate air of nobleness he drew his old cloak closer and prepared to withdraw. He bit his talk; what use to air sorrow? No man cares to accept another's burden, and listening to another's ills is wearisome.

The world's salve, like patent medicine, is for all complaints. Its label is marked "Suffer." It either kills or cures — a blessing on either hand.

As he arose his shoes, leaky, giving glimpses of torn stockings wet with the melting snows, were shuffled backwards to hide their awkwardness, while the parcel was drawn beneath the cloak, and the startled look blotted out on Champlain's chair crept into the eyes, and lit up the olive wrinkles.

"How much is this book?" asked Père Monnier, holding up a well-clad tome.

"*Peut-être*," murmured the count, arresting his footsteps.

"Sell it very cheap," said the bookman, "yes, very cheap, and glad that a man like you will get it. That's a handsome copy, sir—a bargain—an ornament to a library. It is not one of my books, so I can plead and show it off. Open it. Corneille, the great Corneille. Life by Fontanelle. Let me whisper in your ear the price."

"No need, Mr. Thompson, I'll take it at your value."

"*Vraiment?*" uttered the count.

"Perhaps," said the bookseller, "the count

might find in you a purchaser for a few other rare books. Count, this is a Rev. Mr. —— from the States. I was so busy talking of one thing or another that I forgot to ask his name, a sure sign he interested old Thompson."

The count bowed, saying:

"You do me the pleasure to acquaint. I know of your land; it is beautiful, full of intelligence. But the books of it, I have few. Circumstance, monsieur, is very afflicting on me."

He drew out the parcel, untied it, gazed on his last treasures with eyes charged with the heart's electricity. Then said:

"The final of my library. *Voilà*, monsieur," and his head turned away.

"Your old friend Dante," said the bookseller.

"*Oui, oui*, monsieur. I loved him for his pensée, and souvenir of days that will never, never come back to me. While I could keep him I did not feel the douleur of parting with my library, yet it was much to me; but the master was comfort—now adieu, monsieur, you know him who '*sovra gli altri come aquila vola.*' Let me see him again. You will be careful of him; here is a baize to cover him."

"Count," remarked the bookman, "the gentleman may not wish to buy."

"Pardon, pardon," he answered, tapping his forehead; "my emotion makes me forget. Pardon, monsieur; circumstance is sad to me."

"I will buy," said Père Monnier. "Make the price, Mr. Thompson."

"Here it is," said the bookman, handing the père a piece of paper.

"Very, very cheap," said the père. "Here is the money."

"Give it to the count," said the bookseller.

"*Merci! merci!* monsieur," said the count; "you have done me much to-day; my heart is full. *Bon jour.*"

"Strange man," said the bookseller — "a man with a history. Poverty is a leveller, no doubt of that, but as Bobbie Burns says somewhere: 'Nature wrote the man on every feature.' Poverty degrades rogues, not men. The count — well, I must look him up; his books sold, means near the end. I have little to spare, but it's not Thompson to see such a man begging. Begging, did I say? Nonsense! The count beg? He couldn't do it. I must look him up. Men of his stamp die in garrets without a whimper; it's the curs that give tongue."

His moralizing was cut short by Père Monnier's

request to tie up the books, and keep them until he should call.

"All right, reverend," was the blithe reply. The père sallied forth; the bookman eased his mind with a song of home:

> "Symon Brodie had a cow,
>   The cow was lost, and he could na find her;
> When he had done what man could do
>   The cow cam hame, and her tail behind her."

He whistled the chorus, waiting for a new customer.

Père Monnier's brisk walking soon brought him in sight of the count standing in front of a baker's shop, gleeful as a child, snuffing the delicious smells. He could see him draw out the purse and fumble for a coin, make a motion as if to go, then remain still. Were the future and the Brunetaires ominously shaping themselves in his mind? Hunger and honesty gnawed him. His first duty was to pay the irascible Madame Brunetaire. So he moved on, closely followed by the père. He seemed in no great hurry; his homeward journey became a strange roundabout by alleys and small streets. Shabbiness avoids highways and glare. At length he turned into a small street, quickened his pace, until in front of a church door he suddenly stopped, and, leaning against the railing, listened to Gounod's *Ave Maria* stealing through the aisles, melting into the snowflakes around him. As the music died away he entered the church, wending his way slowly, his head down, his heart oppressed by memories, and knelt in front of a little altar by a swinging red lamp. Arising in a few minutes, he piteously looked in the direction of the choir, as if begging for music. None came, save the loose beat of his old shoes on the wooden floor. Down the aisle and out, the wild look blotted from his eyes, the old cloak a little loose, and the old shoes more shown.

"Bless me!" said the père, "this is St. Patrice; but it is long after the dinner-hour, and I'm bound to wind this matter up. It will be a tale worth telling my good friend, and ample apology for an old trick of mine, dinner-missing."

The count had turned a corner, and was now in a shabby, dirty part of Lagauchetière Street. A few steps, he entered an open door decaying on its hinges, mounted a staircase lurched many feet from the wall, its natural support, and was soon lost to view. Père Monnier had his foot on the first step when a shrill, shrieking voice from a little wrinkled mouth shouted in Quebecquois French:

"Monsieur the Count! Come down at once, and pay or get! That's my terms."

All of the commander's person visible at the door was a bit of slippered foot, a wrinkled mouth, a nose, and two gray eyes, cunning as a fox's. Seeing her mistake, she slammed the scarcely open door, shutting shriek and beauty from the well-pleased père. It was Madame Brunetaire on her most orderly parade. Her shriek brought the count from his seclusion. It was a tocsin blast that no inmate could scorn. Bad as it was, the presence of the commander, which followed its disloyalty, was worse. Of two evils the count chose the lesser. Purse in hand, jingling the dollars, sweetest music to soothe madame, music that would wreathe her shattered homeliness with sunny smiles, he left the room and met Père Monnier on the stair. The startled look bounded to his eyes.

"Does monsieur regret his bargain?" he falteringly asked.

"By no means, count; I just came to visit," was heartily delivered by the père. "I take an interest in every man, much more in a countryman and scholar."

"Ah, M. le Curé, you do me the grand honor, but I have it not in my power to receive you. Circumstance is very, very sad to me. I cannot ask you to my chamber—it is most miserable; but I have the grand confidence that I will be better, monsieur; circumstances will not always be cruel to me. It is to me the one grand consolation that the deepest misery has an end. Human douleur goes away with life. Death will cure me. Hear, monsieur, a line from my Corneille: '*Je te l'avoue, mon ami! mon mal est incurable.*' Pardon! Madame calls; she will come. Pardon! she will come."

"Let her," said the père, laughing; "a woman that can let such a shriek is worthy of study."

"I fear she will come. Pardon! monsieur," muttered the count.

"Well," continued the père, "I have a little home, a poor but cosey little church, warm-hearted parishioners, books in all tongues and dresses. I want an organist. You are a musician. Why not come home with me and be a friend and companion, read your Dante, and be as happy as you can? I will settle with madame. You keep your little store. I don't want to recommend myself, but I will say that you will not find me unkind or harsh. Say yes."

The count hesitated. Madame's voice swept the stair, a creaking door told of her coming.

"Say yes," said the père; "the train leaves in an hour."

"Monsieur, *je dis*," rose the madame's voice.

"Say yes," repeated the père.

Tears filled the count's eyes, and stole down his cheeks. He shook his head; Père Monnier read *yes*.

"*Je dis*," said madame.

"*Oui, oui*," laughingly retorted the père.

* * * * *

We are the victims of periodical fads. A few years ago it was haste to the seashore to find health, bathe in the breakers and gain strength. All that has changed. Newspapers—and are not they omnipotent?—declare that the seashore is unhealthy. Microbes hold their annual convention by the loud, roaring sea; colored folk find religion by its surf, and jaunty Jews there elbow too closely mushroom respectability. All things change, as change they must—so goes the song; the popular tune is, Heigh-ho to the mountains. Respectability there has full length to swing its train, and, what is more gratifying, unbridled opportunity to waste its pocketbook. Inducements as these have crowded our mountains with a peculiar class of aristocrats, who quite naturally treat the inhabitants as barbarians. These Greeks, sallow and gaunt for the most part, Sangrado types, swarm on the lakes by day, reading cheap realism in yellow covers, by night singing sentimental songs to the tattered notes of a loose-stringed guitar. We mountaineers laugh a mental laugh, the face as serious as that of a bishop taking his see, use the waste for many a needful thing, hoist ropes, spread tents gladly for these summer circuses. I wrote *gladly;* I was going to explain, but let the word stand while I add, if the pay-car accompanies each show. That is mercenary, you say; tell it to the mountaineer, and, like the traditional Celt, he will respond by asking, "Don't you think, sir, our company's worth something?" On your answer will depend whether you are a Greek or brother barbarian. Père Monnier lived in the mountains, but in a secret nook unknown to the Greeks. There was no noise in the woods save that of pleasantry, singing birds, chattering squirrels, mumbling coons, with not unfrequently the soft musical bleat of the doe calling her fawns to covert and rest. The brooks and lakes were well stocked with fish, and their banks with the wily musk-rat, the saucy minx, and the unsocial otter. The woodsman's axe had not strewn the mountains with giant trees for lumber or pulp-wood; aloft they pointed with all their gracious majesty, true guards of the mountains in their merry green downs. Respectability had not shot the warbling tribe in order to decorate spinsters' hats, nor slaughtered fish to gain the empty name of crack sportsman. Deer were not hurried and worried to death by a mongrel crowd of curs running at fifty cents a day, choice game for those who crowded the lakes and were in as much danger of shooting each other as shooting the dog-run deer. Respectability had not found this nook. She will, but the père will not know of her coming — a blessing for which he earnestly prayed.

* * * * *

Three years had passed—three years of peace and piety for M. le Comte. He had become attached to the père, loved the little, homely, wooden church, and played its organ with as much enthusiasm as in the days when brave men applauded, and fair ladies waited in sunshine and rain to kiss his hand. The parishioners, sturdy fellows and comely women, saw in him a scion of old France — that France long lost, but near and dear to every Canadian heart.

Blood and nobility, even in our plebeian age, count. Monsieur was, as they said, a French Frenchman, and let any of the Yankees come up to him. It was their mode of speaking, a challenge to the saucy Yankee who had so often derided their race and language. Monsieur le Comte was not cold to their warmth. Like most men, he held that blood meant more than water. Canada was the daughter of France; her ways and half-bitten French awoke but memories of the fatherland. He was growing old gracefully, and priest and people were happy dreaming of years and Monsieur le Comte.

It was a summer habit of Père Monnier — habits differ in season — to walk in his garden every evening, reciting the Breviary, now and then bowing to a lily, touching lightly a sweet-briar rose, or watching that bit of sunshine, the golden robin fall from a tree, adding color to a bed of poppies, or listening to his sombre-clad namesake from a leafless maple twig sing sweet roundelays to his brooding spouse. It was M. le Comte's delight, on such occasions, to steal to the organ-loft, after opening every window and door, and touch the keys, sending the spirit of music on hushed wings through the garden, giving a new meaning to flowers, a truer insight to bird-songs, a soul to the Breviary's printed page. How often had Père Monnier tried to give this divine feeling a name! But, baffled, he used this word-language to stimulate his memory, "A subtle something as easy to capture as to define." It is vague, but let the critic be reminded that it is a trifle hard to put your word-drapery on a spirit. In his failure of expression he found comfort quoting Collins' lines:

> "Exalting, trembling, raging, fainting,
> Possesst beyond the Muse's painting."

It was after one of these scenes that Monsieur le Comte, accompanied by a huge mastiff —the parish dog—joined the père.

"Well, well! Yes, well, well!—how prosaic! But that is all the criticism I can sputter out when you play."

"Ah, M. le Curé, it is to me much. The eyes have given to me the best compliments. It is easy to make nice words, but intelligence talks with the eyes. The mouth deceives, the eye — never, never; ignorance or knowledge, M. le Curé, is the flashlight."

They had dropped into a rustic settee, shaded by a huge maple tree.

"That makes me think what an experience you must have had, count, in your life."

"Experience, père, is the motive power in sorrow; sorrows are all experiences." He was using his native tongue. "What is life but a series of experiences? Experience is the fulness of every life; it varies. If you say I had strange experiences, yes; and as I feel so well to-day, to-day so grateful, let me relate one. It will be a commentary to the line from Corneille quoted in those days of misery and Madame Brunetaire; you remember it: '*Je te l'avoue, mon ami! mon mal est incurable.*' The story is short. You are an artist, M. le Curé; I will submit the skeleton, clothe it with flesh, give it blood. It is a reality to me, but I cannot transfer it as it is. I have lived it. It is a part of me in flesh, blood, marrow; to you it can be but the story of a friend. I can put the bones together better standing; emotions want room."

He stood; then, as if narrating the story of another, he said slowly:

"Henri Marie Perryve, Count of Cayla, of illustrious descent, was born in Paris fifty years ago, educated in the province. At an early age he showed great love for music, and was sent to study with the best Italian masters. He became an artist whose fame still haunts the concert-rooms of Europe. After a European tour filled with honor and decorations he returned to France, and wedded his first love, Marie Auguesseu, a famous actress. One of his letters at that time, now faded and torn, would say that this rare artistic union was the height of married bliss. She bore me two children," — he had unconsciously become the actor; — "they haunt me. I cannot see them, but I feel their presence near, or is it a delusion of a mad-wrung brain? Soon will the solution come. I longed to see Canada and the great republic. It was easy to gratify my wish, as managers had long been pressing me to take that trip. I embarked from Havre, with my Marie and her children, bidding a year's adieu to the hundred friends who came to see us depart. It was a long voyage, but we were young, and the children healthful and merry. One night I was awakened by creaking of cordage, cursing, and human wailing. I jumped from my cot and hastened deckward. A quick, dull thump, a lurch—that was all. Some time when in Montreal, if my history interests you, call at the asylum and ask for a record of Count Henry. It begins by my being picked up by the fishing-smack *Halifax*, brought there, and there remaining for years and years. 'Saved' is the record word—hideous word to me. At length little glimmers of reason fused in my mind, until they became strong enough to warrant my keeper's writing on my passport, 'Harmless.' I was free, owner of a little money held in France, and a few rare daily used books that had followed us by the next outgoing vessel from Havre, and had laid boxed for years and years in the cellar of my asylum. No one knew me but Thompson, and misery drove me to him. The money drained day by day, vanished, and my only friends had to go. Poverty is despotic. In my last struggle you came, Père Monnier; Marie and the babies besought the Master, and He sent you, Père Monnier — my own Père Monnier. That is the tale. How easy to box life! I feel a strange sensation. I will compose myself at the organ. List to my music."

He stole away, and soon the garden was sad

and dreamy with sound. Sound begot forms, hope full of joy and life, charity folding her wings over age, faith conquering death.

"Mozart's last requiem," said the père.

A zephyr caught the dying strains, swelled into a breeze, and played a melody with the maple boughs.

"This is his masterpiece," said the père. "I must thank him and soothe him. It is strange that he should delay his story, and this his best, so long from me."

He entered the little church, clambered the stairs that led to the organ-loft, and noiselessly approached the bending count. His long, bony fingers pressed the keyboard, but the spirit that animated them had fled.

"Requiescat in pace!" was the broken sob of Père Monnier.

CHAPTER IX.

PÈRE MONNIER.

SQUIDVILLE had churches, a thriving school, and a post-office, yet she was unsettled and ambitious. Like most mountain towns, she yearned for the airs of city life, and, like the South Sea Islander, donned them by scraps. Talk, that piquant sauce of small places, had set the town agog about a new railway. The railway was a month's sensation, then it grew tiresome, and at length irritating. Folks whistled whenever it was mentioned. "Whistling," said Billy Buttons, "is the easiest way in the world to squelch a gabby-mouthed creature." As a saying it was much in vogue.

Railroad talk having collapsed, something new was essential. "Men cannot gape at each other and say nothing," was another nut from Buttons' wisdom-pile. As a commentary to this Cagy was wont to remark "that men are not ducks, to pop their heads up and down, and then go on." It was a strange remark of mine, hurriedly pencilled in my diary, that deaf and dumb people could not enjoy life in a village like Squidville; seeing everybody talk about every other body, and not being able to enjoy that priceless luxury, they would certainly die. It was Keats who truthfully wrote "that there is not a fiercer hell than in the failure of a great object." What failure can compare with the failure to talk? It was during one of these lulls that bridge sensations that Squidville was put in her usual mood. It came from a new quarter, but that but added to its worth. For years Père Monnier had labored in Squidville. He had seen his flock grow from a dozen families of French and Irish wood-choppers to what he was wont to call a tidy congregation. He had built a neat church, mostly with his own hands, and by his sunny disposition and open-hearted kindness to men of all creeds he had won for himself a niche near the core of all hearts. His scanty purse was ever open to the wants of poverty. On various occasions he was known to give away his boots, and trudge home in his leaky rubbers through the winter's snow, much to the discomfort of Anna, the good old housekeeper, who would solemnly aver that "Père Monnier had a terrible lot of book-sense, but that kind of sense don't go in a town like Squidville, where everybody takes whatever they get, without considering from where it came." Père Monnier, on such occasions, would promise to care for health and pocket in the future, but in the face of poverty and hunger such promises were eagerly forgotten, and the deerskin purse or wearing-apparel was offered in a way that left neither sting nor aching memory in the gift. He had his foibles — most men have. His were on the better side, and with them he had won his way to hearts that held little in common. It was a common sight to see him standing amid his flowers, trowel in hand, pointing to this phlox, or propping that carnation, a bevy of keen-eyed, robust children wondering that his head could contain all it knew.

He loved children with that healthy love that looks at them as the most interesting period, the time of purity and bliss, when the world has not as yet enslaved their hearts with its siren airs. He fully understood the Master's beautiful saying, "Suffer little children to come unto Me." Children intuitively knew this, and flocked to him, delighting to be the lambs of such a shepherd. With gentleness he extracted their manliness, and in their pastimes and games, moving among them, but added to their respect, while it heightened their love. "Be honorable and you'll get along with Père Monnier," was the common say. It was a truth well put. Dogs were his constant companions. A stranger was sure to be told that "his Mickey could water a deer before you would have time to draw your tricker," and the village would confirm this, and proudly add that it was a knowing deer that could fool the père. Guides who had resented what they were pleased to gingerly call dominie influence, admiring Mickey's wonderful skill, came near his master. From that moment harshness and rudeness fled. "I didn't like him at first," said Snappy Woodruff, the worst man that carries a gun in our woods, "but ye have only to rub against him to find the genuine stuff. None of your rotten wood about him." On hearing this Buttons, stamping a letter, fiercely exclaimed: "Snappy gave in his gun, shot right through lungs and liver after saying he wouldn't stand on the same side of the river; that's dropping with the first bullet." Other men, and they were not few, saw in the tall, athletic père a rare scholar, alert to every move that convulses society, and a calm critic, capable of seeing through shams, and pricking them with an irony and sarcasm masterly blended. Such men could not understand why a man of such great gifts, and these so thoroughly developed by study and travel, could spend the best years of his life among an ignorant and poverty-stricken people.

To one who had asked him for an explanation he remarked in his earnest way, his gray eyes lit up: "As it is written: 'For Thy sake we are killed all the day long; we are accounted as sheep for the slaughter.'" Then, raising his voice, and running his long, tapering fingers through his well-mixed hair: "Nay, in all these things we are more than conquerors through Him that loved us." The questioner was gazing at the birds, books, and flowers that peeped from every corner of the cottage. These words withdrew his eyes, and riveted them on the speaker. The face was tranquil, as if the words were the subject of his meditation. "I admire your life; I cannot comprehend your philosophy," was the questioner's muttered response. "And yet it is the only philosophy that can cure your world-pain," was the quiet rejoinder. Such was the man who was to give Squidville its greatest and most lasting sensation. It came, as most sensations, from a small beginning.

It was carefully coddled, watchfully tended; it travelled, grew. To-day it is a part of Squidville's history, and the foundation of this tale. There is a saying that has been handed down the ages. Like most sayings, it is the essence of thousands of individual experiences. It is not a verity under all conditions, but it has been, so many times, that to-day it finds a place in the common wisdom of the people. It runs, "The nearer the church the further from God." It was a verity on this occasion. The nearest house to Père Monnier was occupied by Louis Frechette, a tall, angular Canadian, whose slight shoulder-stoop and long, muscular arms told of a race of wood-choppers. He was a good man blessed with a large family, giving thanks for each new arrival, and singing, "The more the merrier." A few sports were heard to wonder how he could support them. His answer was short and pithy: "The Sender will provide." It was a truth.

The children had plenty; they frisked and gambolled on the green meadows, decked themselves with daisies and buttercups, breathed the keen, health-giving air, and fell asleep, each a prince in the realm of health. They groaned not under the oppression of modern conveniences, nor were they enervated by what we are pleased to call the luxuries of civilization. In truth, they were free from that most abominable tyranny, "the tyranny of things." Dyspeptics, whose yearly pilgrimage to our woods is the new fad; men carrying more fat than they can conveniently handle; lean, lanky, snappy-eyed females, given to women's rights, ignorant of men's wants; and those troubled with insomnia—envied the olive-hued little giants. They would have gladly exchanged their finery and sallowness for the health and appetite of the Frechettes. The children were happy in their station. An exchange could only mean misery. They laughed at "city scarecrows," and rollicked away to the music of bird and brook. Rollicking and the noise it begot was the father's staunch plea each Saturday night "that he had to leave his house for a little rest, or the young ones would drive him crazy." He was honest in his delusion. With constant exertion he had come to believe his plea was genuine. Ordinarily mindful of his wife, he never coupled her with his hobby; perchance he was thinking of a mountain saying, "Every horse a different halter." He acted on his plea, and after supper, admonishing the children "to make less noise when I'm out," he would wend his way to the post-office, where other choice spirits, riders of similar hobbies, came later. The post-master, to make ends meet, kept in a glass case, shoulder to shoulder with mixed candies, a line of long, straw-colored cigars, cheap enough to enjoy after a week of toil. With one of these, spurting and reeking by turns, held in the extended mouth of each, story after story of bear and catamount was boastingly told. Each reciter was the hero of his narrative. Some story suffered when the young Poulets, rapping at their stepfather's office, sang out, " Near morn; and ma can't see why some women don't keep their men at home, hers is lost be them." The postmaster would then laughingly announce: " Woodchucks, to your holes !" The door was locked, and the hardy fellows, in their light jackets, humming some old air brought by their fathers from old France, sauntered home, smiling in the night, asking the stars curious questions. Frechette's pleasant delusion had a serious drawback. On Sundays, when the villagers flocked to their little church, gayly dressed, laughter in the eyes and merriment in the mouth, happy within, no malice without, he slept. It was even hinted by one of his relations that he snored. His children, who caught the birds napping, and without the slightest decrease of prattle, were unable to disturb him. This staggered Buttons, who, no matter when he went to bed, was always the first to greet his pastor. His puzzle was this: he could not understand that the noise that drove a man crazy on Saturday night could make him snore Sunday morning.

Frechette would not be unhorsed to explain. Men rarely choose to analyze their delusions. Frechette's conduct had been passed upon by all church-going women. Stayers at home remembered the adage about living in glass houses. As he slept, he was condemned.

Women suffer from their husband's infirmities. Mrs. Frechette followed the rule. She heard of her spouse's infirmity in a thousand ways, each way a nettle-sting. Human endurance has a limit. In her misery she sought her pastor, and asked for a cure. It was to come from Père Monnier, without a hint of her interference—one of the ways that love conquers all things. The père had but one salve for all such ills; it was labelled KINDNESS, and rarely failed to cure the sore. One Sunday morning service was late. Rumor, that talkative old dame, gathering the worshippers in little groups, gave to each of them a different explanation. While they listened to her prattle Père Monnier stood by the bedside of Louis Frechette, appealing to his better nature. The appeal was debated. Frechette, as usual with mountaineers, argued from nature. His point most dogmatically asserted was "that everything sleeps until it wakes." Behind this to his mind impregnable fortress he lay. Another rampart was "that it was the business of churches to have bells to get the folks around in time, and any minister that don't bell his church is doing wrong, according to the Canada belief." Half rising in his bed, he exclaimed: "Père, put a bell on the church; sound her in the morn, the way they do in Canada. Give us a chance, folks that have no rooster-clocks to cackle in our ears, and I warrant you I'll be there before Billy Buttons."

"A bell! ay, a bell!" whistled the père.

"Yes, a bell! a bell!" more strongly and firmly retorted Frechette. "All the folks are talking about her; they're wild for her—ready to pop their names on paper, but you won't do the asking." Pulling an old deer-skin bag from under the pillow, he unfastened it, and from one corner of it, tucked away for years to bolster a pet theory, he drew a five-dollar gold piece, and with eyes of almost ecstatic joy, and hand trembling with long pent-up emotion, he muttered: " Pop me first for a five; pop me two times if some of them don't toe the scratch. I'll die happy when I hear her going it. That's all the town wants, and you're the man to give her, eh, père? Well, well! just to hear her playing out a bit of a tune, one of these fine frosty mornings, will make me a lad again. I wish you could get the mate of her, where I came from." Youthful memories are the relish of later life.

Père Monnier clasped his hands, and hurried to his church. The villagers read something in his face. Not a few said that " there were tracks of new-made tears." The hidden something was unbosomed when after service he announced, in his own sweet way, that he was to blame for not studying the wishes of his flock as regards a bell. There was a nodding, and a steady working of eyes; even the youngsters scratched their heads, that ancient sign-board of wisdom. " He could not head the subscription; that was already done by one who would not allow his name to be given. He would from his scanty salary gladly subscribe, be the second signer. Who would follow?" The sensation took life. It was dual. Who blamed the père? Who was the first signer? It disdained creeping, grew, and for years distanced all competitors. The rapid signing of names, with the promise to pay as soon as logging commenced, convinced Père Monnier that Frechette but spoke the temperature of the people's pulse when he said "that all the folks are talking of her; they're wild for her, ready to pop their names on paper."

Snow came, wages were good, and the Squidvillites, true to their promises and signatures, deposited in the hands of Père Monnier an adequate sum to place a little bell on their church. If it could be up for New Year's Day, was the common byword. Billy Buttons was not slow to carry the people's wish to the père, He returned with the news that by Christmas she would "be going it as well as ever she would in her life. If not, might he never see a deer." This gave his information the seal of truth. When we vow by the loss of the things we love even scepticism is silenced. This pleasing news gave new life to Frechette. Believing Buttons, he would nevertheless hear from a more authentic source the glad tidings. Père

Monnier, a lover of nature, sat in his cosey sitting-room, surrounded by flowers and singing birds, by times gazing at his Dante, at others listening to the storm scudding the snow-dust in its wake, or watching the wind-wrung trees disrobe. He was at peace, happy in his life among the poor and poverty-stricken. He was consoled in hardships by the deep, earnest love they bore him. What was the city's glitter and jangle, masking hypocrisies, hypocrisies that such a nature as his would easily prick, to those rough but loyal hearts? The book seemed to whisper that his was the true environment to study the cold Ghibeline's immortal poem. The birds and flowers flitted into his dream. Shutting his eyes to crystallize into one form all these speaking things, he muttered, "It is good to be here." The door-bell rang, a hearty, whole-souled noise disturbing Anna's nap over a batch of cookies, and opening the mastiff's huge jaws in a gruff rejoinder.

"Enter," said the père, and the smiling face of Louis Frechette graced the little sitting-room.

"A bustling day, père. The snow is running like a greyhound, but it will soon stop its cantering. It may leave a few drifts—nothing to bother you, père. We were saying that you're getting to be quite a horseman since you took to these roads. Yes, says I, and may you be long spared on them. I wish we could only do a little more for you, but, as Jemmie Barbier says, if wishes were things the divil wouldn't have many in his company below. Here's another five to help to buy the bell-rope. You forgot to put that in your announcer. You might as well have Poux the dummy in your tower as a bell without a rope tied to its clapper. I might have waited a few days, but I heard that you were going away to-morrow to get her; so my wife says, ' Louis, you had better be giving that money to the père.' That's so, says I, so up I steps. I must be getting back. I was in a hurry, so I came without fixing myself. Well, a poor man cannot be too fidgety about his clothes. Get her as good as you can; that you'll do, I'll warrant. Good-night, mon père."

The door was quickly shut, and the wiry form of Frechette, incased in a ragged snow-robe, was homeward bound. Père Monnier, impelled by the rough goodness of such a man, opened the door to get another look at the wood-chopper. The snow had curtained off all visible things; the wind brought him back a chanson:

> "Vive la Canadienne,
>   Vole, mon cœur, vole;
>   Vive la Canadienne,
>   Et ses jolis yeux doux,
>   Et ses jolis yeux doux,
>   Tout doux,
>   Et ses jolis yeux doux."

It was a favorite with his mother, and for the memory of her to whom the nobleness in his nature belonged he continued the song, much to Anna's chagrin, and the total destruction of the cookies. With a sigh of relief she beheld a horseman come to the door, dismount, and pull the bell. Père Monnier hurriedly answered the call, and read the message in the bearer's face: "Some of your folks are sick, John?"

"Yes, père, my wife and three children, desperately bad. I am on my way for the doctor; but you said you should be called in such a case as soon as him. Anyway, they want to see you. I hate to bring you out,— roads are bad, as well as the night,— but I know you always told us that you would rather be with the sick than the well."

"Don't mind excuses, John; it's only duty. I am only too happy to go. If the doctor refuses to come tell him that I will see that he gets his pay."

"O père! père! père!" was the only answer. Tears had broken his speech. His sorrow pressed lighter. He raised his head, gazed long at Père Monnier. Love glistened among tears.

A few minutes after his departure Père Monnier rode out of his yard, patting Molly, and promising her an extra feed if she would carefully pick her way. The animal was willing, expressed by a neigh, so away they went for a twenty-mile journey. Following the highway for a few miles, Père Monnier struck into a narrow road leading through a spruce and pine forest, and opening into a hilly, sandy tract dotted with huge boulders. Here rose a few scattered huts. Before one of them a lantern burned, a sure sign it was the sick-house. Riding up, he dismounted, put his horse in a rickety shed, throwing his buffalo-coat over him. Pulling the latch-string, he entered. There was a subdued greeting, and a hurried whispering among the few neighbors that it was a miracle how Père Monnier "got through the woods." In his honor a new lantern was lighted and held in a corner of the house. By it a woman in the last stages of consumption was visible, lying on a rough pallet of chaff. In the opposite corner was a half-broken bedstead, propped up by a row of cord-wood. There lay two children, wan and emaciated, wrapped in a few old coats and a faded horse-blanket. The mother stretched out her long, fleshless fingers as a welcome. The marriage-ring fell on her pallet; it had been long since unable to find a hold. The eyes of the little sick ones became brighter; even the baby, held in a neighbor's arms, stopped its natural but weird cry of "ma, ma." The coming of a good man availeth much, is a saying of mine. Soon a tale of woe fell on his patient ear, first by the garrulous neighbors, then by the broken, sobbing voice of the dying woman. The little ones punctuated the tale by sharp pain-cries. The tale was but a chapter of sorrow in that long book, so thoroughly known to him, the history of human suffering. Although it was evident that no human effort could lengthen the sufferer's life, yet she could be comforted, consoled, and her children saved.

"When is the mortgage due, Mrs. Livernois?" asked Père Monnier, gently holding her hand, while watching the sunken, glassy eyes.

"In a few days, père. And he is as good as his word; he will put us out. We have sold everything, as you see; nothing left but me and the young ones, and we won't be with John long. Where we are going we'll need neither house nor food. It's different with John,— poor fellow! how he struggled,— but—" The woman's voice sank to a whisper, and died in a long, drawn-out sob.

"True for you, Mrs. Livernois; he is as good as his word."

"We know that," broke from the neighbors' lips.

Cruelty leaves a lasting impression. Long after its obsequies its shadow is a torment; its scar never heals. Père Monnier was practical— true charity always is. Hunger is a poor listener to beautiful phrases. Once relieved, it is docile. Some of Frechette's bell-rope money was handed to a neighbor to buy the necessary groceries. A little sum was left in the bony hand of Mrs. Livernois. "And as to the dreaded mortgage," said Père Monnier, "I will settle that with Gregg. You must not worry about it. By the way, I have a spare bed — just the thing you want. Some of the neighbors can come and get it—the quicker the better."

There was a silence. All eyes were upon him in whose coming came mercy. As he left the house and struck the bridle-path he could not help ejaculating: "Dispossessed from these stones! Of all animals man's cruelty is the most developed."

He knew Josiah Padlock Gregg too well to ask a further stay. He was troubled as he thought of his promise to the sick woman, and not a copper in his house save the bell-money. At that moment the story of Abraham and Isaac floated through his mind: "God will provide." No sooner had he reached home than he dispatched Anna to Gregg with the bell-money.

That worthy while counting the money retold the story of Livernois, and ended it by warning Anna that her master must have plenty of money "to prop up such skinflints as John Livernois and his brood." Selfishness regards charity as a fool. Anna's mind was agog. "Merciful goodness! had he given the bell-money? What would happen?"

Every step was convincing. Gregg had expressed a hope that a bell might be upon the church some time "before the coming of Gabriel." She would use this as a means of drawing out Père Monnier. Her ordinary walk, a waddle of the tame-goose sort, became a trot. Curiosity is the fruitful mother of worry. Panting, she arrived at the parsonage. Her master opened the door with "You have paid Gregg and brought me the mortgage?"

"Yes, père; but he talked about nothing but a bell. He doubts its ever going up."

A shadow crossed the good man's face. It was for a moment; then he answered: "Anna, God will provide."

She hurried to the kitchen, shaking her head. Her heart was heavy; her eyes were wet. "The bell-money was gone. What would Père Monnier do?"

Day after day passed, Anna noticing a change in her old master. His books were forgotten; the birds and flowers unnoticed. He sat by his desk, writing and writing. She could hear that dreary pen pass over the paper hour by hour. He was as pleasant and as charitable as in the olden time, but somehow or other the old smile was wanting. The writing became less constant. She could hear him read, stop, leave his desk, walk his room, return, and then the dreary sound of the pen. "Poor man! he's killing himself to make bell-money," was her say. One day the writing ceased. Père Monnier was unable to leave his bed. "A little cold," he said, "that would soon pass; he would be well in a day or two." Anna knew better, so, despite his remonstrances, the doctor came, felt his pulse, chatted awhile, shook his head, as we physicians are wont to do, and whispered in Anna's ear, "Pneumonia." The news soon spread. It was the only topic at the Hunter's Paradise. Among those who listened to the many tales of his generosity, drawn forth by his sickness, was Miss Barton Inglis, who had lately arrived for the deer-hunting season. She had that day paid a visit to her old guide, Livernois, and there learned what Père Monnier "had done for him and his."

"I must, Mr. Weeks, see this man before I return."

"I shall go with you, Miss Inglis," said the proprietor. "I know Père Monnier for a good many years. I am proud to say he slept his first night under my roof. If you could only wait a few days, until he is up and around. I know you will enjoy your visit."

One evening Anna's dreams were rudely dispersed by the entry into her kitchen of James Weeks and a young lady whom she knew to be "a city folk." The lady shook her hand, asked for Père Monnier, and acted as if she had, to use Anna's phrase, "been bred and born in the house." Weeks, after depositing some little things that his old friend might relish, retired, leaving the two women in close conversation. "Now, Anna, tell me," said the younger, "what is the cause of Père Monnier's sickness." After many warnings not to repeat, the story of the bell "that should be up by Christmas," but now, as Gregg says, "won't be up to Gabriel's day," was told.

"I have a plan, Anna," said Miss Inglis. "You will nurse the père; get him well. Such a man must live; we need him. During his recovery I will have a belfry built, and a bell ready to ring in Christmas."

"I think the ringing," said Anna, "would make him be himself again."

"You must keep the secret, Anna."

Tears ran down her cheeks. To her honor be it written, with many tongue-bites she succeeded.

Père Monnier's sickness was long and hard. Within a few days of Christmas a change for the better came. A new priest had come to conduct the service. To him the père deputed the task of explaining the delay in the bell. He was not to spare Père Monnier, and to finish with the promise of having it as soon as the père was able. Christmas Eve came, long and lonely for the sick man. The little church was beautifully decorated with soft mountain evergreens, and the little crib, built many a month ago by his own hands, lent a quaint if sad charm. He could hear the sleigh-bells merrily ringing, and the happy voices of the children. How he longed to be with them! He would form a picture of his little flock, and pray for the peace which the world could not give them. Picture after picture came. He went by the altar—the altar one blaze of light, encircled by the dark green of cedar and spruce —pleading for his people. The choir was singing "Bethlehem." His eyes became weary, his head heavy; he struggled a moment to hold his dreams, then softly slept. He suddenly awakes; it is striking twelve. Was he dreaming? What sound is that? It fills the air, and bears joy into each household. It sends greeting to all. Hear it again! He feels his head. Still louder and louder it rings over the snow-covered vales, and dies away in far-off mountain caves. "His head—his weary head!"

Tears run down his cheeks. "Is reason gone?" Still louder and louder it calls Père Monnier to health, and tells the love of his people. Frechette holds the bell-rope. It stops. A wild cheer rends the air. His room is thrown open, and a dozen voices tell him the tale of the Squidville bell.

The traveller of to-day who visits Squidville's lonely churchyard will find a grave on the brow of the hill, guarded by the spreading branches of a giant maple. There is a well-tracked path to the grave. In summer-time this grave is covered with daisies, buttercups, and roses—children's gifts.

There is a marble monument in the shape of a bell, and on it this curious inscription:

Sacred

To the Memory

of

Père Monnier.

"Christ's lore and His Apostles' twelve
He taught, but first he followed it himself."

Erected

by

CHARLES, JAMES, AND JENNY LIVERNOIS,

Children

of

JOHN AND FROZINA LIVERNOIS.

CHAPTER X.

HOME AT LAST.

PASSENGERS coming to our town came by the stage; whenever any other conveyance was used it became noteworthy and a subject of talk. When, then, one fine summer morning a spanking pair of bays, drawing a fashionable carriage containing a lady and a child, drove up to the Hunter's Paradise, there were few of us that did not take a stroll in that direction.

I cannot deny but curiosity was at the bottom, nor am I going to condemn myself for giving way to a feeling which has prompted our race in all ages to marvellous adventures. Without it how wanting would our lives be, especially in a mountain town! So curiosity keeps away dulness. By the time I had reached the hotel the lady and her child had alighted, and were superintending the transfer of their baggage. I took a seat on the piazza, interested in the new-comers.

The lady seemed to eye the hotel curiously.

As her gaze rested on the piazza I had a fairly good shot at her face, which was young and beautiful. There was something in the face known to me that set me rummaging amid old memories.

"Well," said Buttons, who had joined me, "Weeks is going to have some trade. That's an elegant rig. I wonder if she wants a guide? Things are dull in the lettering business; I could leave it for a couple of weeks to one of the youngsters if I could get a soft snap. I ain't as young as I used to be, that's sure; but I am spry enough to guide any lady, no matter how active she be. It's no harm to be ahead for the job, so I'll ask Weeks."

"Billy," said I, "does she remind you of anybody you have ever seen? Her face is familiar; yet who she is, or from whence she comes, I can't collect myself enough to know. Well, there goes Jim, smiling as usual. How he manages to keep so light-hearted is my puzzle."

"It's only on the surface; the heart's ate out years ago," said Buttons, "ay, years ago. How can it be otherwise?—neither child nor chick left him. You see only the bark, and the use of that is for hiding. 'Tis as Père Monnier says, the coffin—the corpse is inside.

"Now I get a good sight on her, yes, that face is powerfully natural to me, but I'm poking my memory for a name.

"What eyes—black as jet! regular daggers! That's as handsome a face as ever struck these parts. Well, now it does look like some face that I have seen years ago. It may take a long time to cipher it out, but I'll get it or lose my night's sleep. Here she comes; get a good look at her, doctor."

The lady, holding the child's hand, was soon in front of us, smiling very pleasantly.

"Doctor," said Weeks, "this is Mrs. Minton, from Chicago. She wishes to be introduced to you and Buttons. She says she has heard of you; and who in thunder does not know Billy? The lady tells me she has been here before. That beats me; I must be losing my memory. Once I was good in remembering faces. Buttons, you know everybody who comes here: can you guess the lady?"

"Jim," said Buttons, "it's mighty queer; I can't for my life. Yet me and the doctor were saying there's something very familiar in that same face. It's like an old letter you stick away somewhere. You know of it, but you can't just place it on the minute. I have seen them eyes in one woman, God rest her soul!" and Buttons raised his hat. "She was a good woman at that, one of the best; as Cagy put it, 'Her likes will never be seen round these diggings again.' She is over there, ma'am," pointing in the direction of the little graveyard, "these many a days, sleeping where we'll all sleep some day."

A large, reeky tear hastily ran down Buttons' cheek. He was unaware that his simple words had a like effect on the lady.

Weeks, dreaming of his own sorrows, was making a desperate effort to conceal his emotion.

I was not indifferent, but somehow or other the sorrows of man have long since ceased to draw my tears. Amid such scenes I am possessed with a gentle melancholy, and not infrequently have caught myself muttering these strange lines of Shelley:

> "All things that we love and cherish,
> Like ourselves, must fade and perish."

"I am that woman's daughter," said the lady, pressing a handkerchief to her eyes; "that woman's daughter come back to see a mother's grave, and those who were kind in the black, gnawing days of adversity so long ago."

"It's all like a dream to me," said Weeks, "all like a dream. To think that little Aily should be in my house, grown big, married at that; ay, what's more, having a youngster of her own, as like her grandmother as two peas. I'm right glad to see Aily; couldn't be prouder if it was one of my own—but in a kind of a way you are, as I brought up your father. I take it that you have, as we say, struck luck. It was very hard for me to see your father going out West, but it was all for the best. Squidville is a poor place; we live, nothing more. But come in, Aily—pardon my being so familiar, but old Weeks would like to be close to your father's daughter. I heard you call the little tot Milly; do you tell me that's her name? Well, well, what memories float into my old skull! I must take the tot in my arms and alarm the whole house who's come. While you stay you'll be boss here, and we'll have a gay old time dancing attendance on you."

Clasping the eagerly listening child in his burly arms, he hastened to prepare a meal for the little Aily who had covered him with kisses and mumbled promises on that dreary day when her father, broken-hearted, clasped his cabin door for the last time, and set out for the West to find a home and fortune in a new land. Happiness he craved not; that was buried with his wife in the lonely little mountain graveyard. As he became rich and polished men wondered why some woman would not find in him a loving partner. They knew him not; nor could they know that by his Milly's grave on the day of his departure he had knelt with his child, and in his rough way vowed that "no woman should lord it over Milly's child." He could love but once; and, the link broken, he lived for Aily, each day finding in her something of the Milly he had lost.

At his death he had but one wish: that he should be carried back and laid by the side of his wife, with a little tombstone marked, "Home at last." It was "to have no other squivering upon it." In his last battle business friends were forgotten; his wish was to lie among the friends of his youth until the angel's trumpet should wake the Adirondacks.

It was to fulfil this pious duty that Aily returned to her early home.

As she stood there one could easily dream that it was Milly, the village favorite.

Buttons was dreaming so as he muttered: "Milly, Milly, and is it you?"

"Is Aily forgotten?" asked the lady, rousing Buttons from his dreams. Don't you remember your little girl, Billy Buttons? One of my father's last sayings was, 'Aily, don't let anybody put me beside your mother but Weeks, Cagy, Buttons, and the doctor; they'll do it gently. Before they clay me for good I want Père Monnier to say a few prayers, just a few. He's pretty old, but as he married me, and shut your mother's eyes, I want him to do the last turn for me. Then, before coming away, get his blessing, and show him little Milly, and tell him I have lain many a night in the West thinking what he done for me and everybody else.'"

"Ah, the père is old, Aily!" said Buttons, his eyes becoming wet, "old, Aily; he is not long for us, but I want to lay down my own burden before he goes. I have been all through the war, and didn't bother much; but I'm now a kind of lonely, so that when I come to fire my last shot I would be a bit easier if the père was around. But I must hurry up; the père is near the end. I saw him going up to Cagy's yesterday, just creeping along, holding his stick on the ground to give him a lift. 'My!' says I, 'I knew you when you could climb a hill faster than a deer, and jump at the first go-off any fence in these parts.' It was mighty sorrowful thinkin'; it made me sit down on a stump and feel as if I wanted to sink there on the spot. I'm not much on the tear business,—it was always a kind of soft to a fellow of my turn,—but when I see him hobbling along like a deer wounded in the hind end, and then thought of how he used to run, no matter how I squeezed my eyes the water came fussing down my cheeks, and pretty hot at that."

"Is Cagy sick?" said Aily.

"Well," continued Buttons, "you can't call him just well, or he wouldn't be in bed a minute. Whenever he gives in his gun deuce a much shot he has left. It's never been his way to lie down and sputter with a toothache. When he's down it's a tarnation blow that has struck him, keep that afore you. Mind, I don't say he's never going to reclaim his gun; it looks by his talk as if he would. 'Buttons,' says he, 'this is the first year in fifty that I haven't loosened up a deer with a bullet, but we'll soon have a whack at them.' That's not dying talk, but then Cagy won't say 'die' until he's a prisoner. I wouldn't wonder but your coming would speed him a bit. If he's alive, even if he's carried, he'll help to put your father away in his own lot, and that's the best in the graveyard."

"The best, Billy! That would be kindness itself. But as we like to follow father's last injunction, it will be necessary to bury him with my mother, in her lot, if there is a place there. I trust there is room enough."

"Yes, Aily, there's room and to spare; but you and me are talking of the very same place. When you went West Cagy bought the plot; I went with him to do it. 'Billy,' says he, 'Frank's going cuts my heart. I was just a-looking over the fence at Milly's grave; it's uncommonly lonely, Buttons.' Just then I saw him wiping his eyes, for the first time in years. 'Uncommonly lonely, Buttons,' he went on, 'and what's worse, I don't know what stranger may be planted in it. That's what makes me thaw a bit. You have your own piece and don't want this, else I'd give you the first chance; but I kind of want a place after my jigs are over to take my long nap, and it strikes me it wouldn't be bad policy to buy the lot, and get my certifier. A fellow like me don't want to sleep nigh folks he'll have to be introduced to when Gabriel sounds the horn. Besides, it's next to your hole, so that when the great creeping-out comes, as in old times, we'd shoulder the burden together. At any rate, we could have a quiet word on the situation.' I never saw Cagy so strange-looking as that day. So up we steps to Père Monnier and got our certifier, and Cagy, putting three thicknesses of brown paper around it, put it in a mink-skin bag and hung it about his neck, where he carries it to-day. That give him the title; so he fixed it good and as handsome as a June rose, put iron rods and chains all around, and that was not all. One day he says: 'Do you know the hardest drive I ever got? It was when La Flamme said, "Some day Aily and I might have money enough to buy Milly a headstone." It's a good many years ago. I suppose they ain't on the ups, and they will never come. Well, I have ordered a bit of stone to be put there. I wouldn't let them letter it much. Just Milly's name; if her own ever come back they can fill it in.' So up went the stone. He was proud of it, and in summer evenings after work he would walk out there to weed, train, or water all kinds of flowers he had growing on your mother's grave. If there's anything against Cagy lying there he's not the man to sneak in where he's not in his place, and he knows he's welcome to the best spot I have—no mistake, Aily. Cagy will give you his certifier; but if there's room, better let him nest in the tree of his choosing."

Tears had long been chasing each other on the soft cheeks of Aily. She had often heard her father in the long winter nights talk of Cagy and his strange way. One of those stories came to her bit by bit. She could see her father's face and the queer curve to his lips. His voice was ringing in her ears, saying: "Cagy felt bad the morning we left. He carried you to the station, Aily, weeping like a child. Now and then he would mutter, 'I have been through the mill.' While we were waiting for the train he told me something that was staggering, if it had been at any other time. He had been married when but a youth, but, as he spoke it, 'After marriage I had to come to the States for work. I was to send for Felina, my wife, in a couple of months. Well, before that time was up, breaking her heart about me, she went to a better country. I was on my way home when I heard the news. I returned and never wanted to see my old home. They had clayed for good all that was dear to me. Like yourself, I must wait, perhaps for years, until I see her. That's how I left Canada never to return. I struck up with Buttons here, so I have been pegging away ever since, with a big black load on my heart that nobody could lift, much less make light. I promised to be Felina's, and when the end comes along I won't be looking around, like these fellows that marry two or three times, to see which of the mates I'll be tackled with.'"

This story that Buttons had told her made her uneasy to see the loyal heart, true in love and friendship, strange only to those who knew it not.

"Can we not see Cagy at once?" she was going to say, when Buttons arose and the bell rang merrily out the dinner-greeting of the Hunter's Paradise.

Milly, holding Weeks' hand, now on the most friendly terms with him, was calling her. She went.

That night—news travels rapidly—it was the talk of every fireside, the death and coming burial of all that was earthly of Frank La Flamme. His history was passed from mouth to mouth, and the best in him brought to the surface. Death brings to us many fine things utterly ignored in life.

Squidvillites were proud of him, that, despite wealth, he had never forgotten them, had their memory green in his memory, and dying wished to sleep among them in the little graveyard he had helped as a boy to clear. Nor was his wife forgotten--the village beauty, the patient wife who had been lying all those long, dreary years facing the big black cross, waiting for the only man of many who tried to win her girlish heart. Any failings—and no man is free—were overlooked, and the young were asked to learn a lesson in true love from the hearse and bay horses that were to drive through the village next morning. Widows who had married again for once had little to say. Youth, humming songs of love, scorned any compromise, and spoke only of lasting fidelity.

It became a saying which took root in the village, and was often subsequently used by youth with the land of love very near, and yet not within grasp, " As faithful as La Flamme." On various occasions it had the desired effect of converting wavering maidens to cast their fates with ambitious youths.

In a little maple grove, visible from the Hunter's Paradise, lived William Cagy, better known to fame as Blind Cagy, from the loss of his left eye — a loss that was his boast, and gave to his nickname a title of honor. Strange as it may seem, it was a bit of pure affection in behalf of Squidville that was accountable for the dropping of William and the giving of Blind—a change, here be it remarked, that was satisfactory to all parties.

When the news was first bruited in Weeks' that a war was on hand Cagy, then a mere stripling, was heard to remark "that he had no personal dislike to Jeff." The names of great men were all familiarly treated by the Squidvillites. "But if old Horace was a-getting hot about it he feared there was something in it that didn't just look right; but, anyhow, he would wait for Horace's second toot, which should be due that night."

The *Tribune* brought it, and Weeks, sitting on a cracker-barrel, his hearers on empty soapboxes, elbows leaning on their knees, hats brushed back for a better view, faces eagerly peering into Jim's, heard that spectacled worthy read what was allowed to be "a tarnation hot bit of writing — chunky and collopy, and as gritty as an oak-knot."

"There will soon be the deuce to pay," remarked the reader, finishing with a knowing head-shake; "when old Horace whoops it in that style it's a-gettin' ready for the hunt you ought to be, boys. There's music a-brewing, and the dance is about to be called."

"I hear," said Jed Parker, "that they're recruitin' in Malone, or at any rate they've tooted a call for to-morrow by ten — that's what I heard; and seein' Horace a-going it at that gait makes the thing pretty certain. Well, little I thought their foolin' would come to this; but, as Horace says, the die is cast, flesh will fly and blood flow before the end of this, and many a woman and child have wet eyes."

Just then Cagy became uneasy and whispered something in young Buttons' ear. That youngster nodded and winked, and then both withdrew.

"It's bad policy to read when the youngsters are around," was Weeks' word.

"They're off to the front, I'll bet my life," said old Jed, blaming his sputtering tongue, "that blabbed about the Malone meeting."

Jed was right; the first man to step up at that meeting was Cagy, young Buttons a close second. In Buttons' homely phrase, "They wanted to be sent where they could see some game."

They had their wish. Buttons returned unscathed to tell the valor and grit of the Johnny rebs. Cagy left a finger at Yorktown and an eye at Vicksburg uncomplainingly.

With his home-coming his name was changed. The money he brought tied up in his deer-skin purse bought a maple strip, made a clearing, and erected a neat, cosey log cabin. Time and patience and a never-ceasing watchfulness had twined trailing vines in many a pretty design, making in summer-time the cottage one strange-looking flowering shrub. The garden, with its useful vegetables, was merrily lit up by bits of phlox, beds of poppies, and patches of portulaca. Birds, well knowing the occupant's love for their music, and the perfect safety that was found in the maple grove, came early and lingered late. Even in snow-time one has remarked, "They only changed their coat to fit the frost and homed with Cagy."

The cabin was substantially furnished; the walls decorated with pictures of Lincoln, Grant; Sheridan on his charger, right over Cagy's bed, where he might "have a peep at Phil every morning"; Sherman; and a strange face in that company, as Squidville in her ultramontane patriotism was not slow to point out: it was

Robert Lee. No amount of argument or invective could make Cagy listen to the invitation to "plaster over that with another picture." To such remarks he had but one argument, driven home by hitting his closed fist against the nearest piece of woodwork and spitting through his teeth:

"Plaster Lee's face! Don't try that, friend. Lee may have been on the wrong track, as many a one before him, and a lot behind him will be, but I guess he thought he was as right as we be. That's neither here nor there now; we're all one, if them flabbergasted politicians would leave us alone. As for Rob Lee, he was a man, and a man's face, in these days of pygmies and sneaks, is welcome; so when Rob comes down out of that it will be the day after they carry Cagy out for good."

Somehow or other Squidvillites looking at that face softened in after years.

On the window-sill was a large Bible, referred to by its owner as "the wonderful Book of God, containing a bit of balm for every wayfarer's ill." It was large, bound in calf-skin, big type, full of pictures, a treasure from old France brought by some fighting ancestor and bequeathed to the eldest son in every family. It was always marked by the owner's "one-glassed" spectacles, as the neighbors called them.

There were a few other books, yellowish leaved and blotted from long thumbing, their covers very thick from many coatings made to keep them "in readin' condition."

Their outside told no tales, but a learning-hungry stepson of Buttons found in Cagy's absence "that they were the novels of Walter Scott," and when he bore this information to the Hunter's Paradise there was commotion, and a well-ventilated opinion that Cagy's head " was cracked to be puttering away his time in such silly stuff."

It was also hinted that the blind eye pulled on some of his brain-strings when the folks remembered how often they had seen him by the river-bank, lying under a maple, with a sodded stone for a pillow, "readin' contentedly one of them books, his one eye stuck into the print for hours, heeding nothing around, as if every thing was dead." Even his dog "smelled the rat," and lay at his feet like a cat by the side of a mouse-hole.

The last fireside to hear the news, which was owing to sickness, was Cagy's. A cold that came of a wetting while mail-driving had settled on his chest, and although he had tried to conquer it with a concoction of cream-of-tartar and maple-syrup, "drunk as hot as you could stand it," and fought it with all the grit he had, the battle was unequal.

The mail-route had to be given to less experienced hands, while Cagy by degrees was forced to keep within his cabin, and finally forced to bed. He was bolstered up, his candle on a sconce of his make, his one eye gleaning the adventures of Rob Roy, his heart pattering with sympathy.

It was characteristic of him to have a kindly feeling "for daredevils," as his expression ran.

The fire burned well, a chattering pine log throwing a yellowish light over the walls, lighting up the pictured warriors, and shining on skins of otter, mink, bear, guns, fishing-rods, etc., things which indicated his life-foibles.

The dog that lay in front of the fire, now and then grinning at a flying spark lighting on his body, started to his feet, shook himself, ran to the door, scratched it, then jumped on his master's bed and gave a well-pleased bark. Rob Roy was carefully marked with the one-eyed glasses, and gently buried in the clothes. There had never been a lock or bolt to Cagy's door.

All that was necessary to give it, said the neighbors, "was a shove and it opened itself."

Soon there was a feet-coming and the accustomed shove, and the loud, merry voice, so long known to Cagy, of Billy Buttons.

Time had worsted Billy badly, stooped his back, whitened his head, wrinkled his face, stiffened his limbs, but the voice was as young as the first time it fell on Cagy's ears, capturing him. That cheery voice was the spokesman of a heart that every Squidvillite vowed "was as soft as a girl's, as fine as silk, and when it come to stand up for what was right the bravest in the town."

Cagy, in speaking of Buttons' heart, had always to wipe his eyes when he came to that part of his story where, upon losing his eye, Buttons said, as he kept on firing, "Cagy, old boy, I wish it was my eye, or, for that matter, my two, they knocked out, and let you go; but cheer up, they couldn't kill you by putting an eye out. There's more before you."

That was consoling, and on Cagy's part a memory that did honor to Buttons' heart.

"Man alive! Cagy, is it in bed ye are, and the whole town about crazy? Above all the men you're wanted, and it's in bed ye are,

Think of that! But leaving foolin' go, are you laid up for awhile, or is it something that's a-working off?

"Well, Billy," and Cagy pulled himself up, putting his knees on a line with his head, "it's a cold that I'm trying to syrup out, but it sticks like a burr, and there's no telling how long I may be here."

"You'll be up soon," said Buttons, impatient to communicate the strange news he held—"soon, Cagy. But do you know who's come to town? Well, you don't, or who could, for that matter, unless they were witches? I'll never say again that anything is strange. Little Aily La Flamme is down at Weeks'; full woman, married at that, and has a youngster into the bargain. Why, she's the dead spit of her mother, and you know what that was—the same nose, same eyes, and the same way of throwing back her head. Well, you're looking at me. I don't wonder a bit; and I have more wondering in store for you. She comes on a sad business,"—there were tears in both men's eyes,—"sad business for you and me, Cagy. She comes to bury her—"

"Father. Billy!" said Cagy, clearing his eyes with the sheet, "that's the end of us all; but

I'm glad that Frank came back to Milly. She was lonely, Billy, so lonely that I thought of keeping her company; but now that her rightful partner has come back I'll be content anywhere you put me—of course, the nearer my chums the better. Perhaps you could spare a bit of your ground. You and I have been pretty close in life, and I kind of hate to get away from you."

He was fingering a little bag that hung around his neck, and from it he drew his "certifier" and handed it to Buttons.

"That belongs to Aily. I just kept it, waitin' for her. I'm only sorry that the stone is so poor. I suppose they will put in its place something grand, like what we've seen during the war; but I'll never see it, and I'm just as glad. That little bit—I have seen it so often—it has got close to me, and no big affair could take its place."

"Man, you're a-talking as if you had given up the hunt. When you drop, Cagy, we'll plant you beside Milly and Frank. That's Aily's way of concocting it. But you're not getting any of those quavers in your skull? Never say die; a cold won't drop you; it will take a few of them new-fangled diseases that the doctors spout out without drawing a breath to knock you over. You're good for a hundred.

"Now, the funeral will be to-morrow; so, if you can, you're coming.

"Come to my house and have a bit of something early; then you and I will creep over to Weeks', where there will be a team and Aily waiting for us. She's full of you; and maybe I didn't tell her what you had done; and you needn't be shaking your skull, it was right. I don't believe in letting a man die before I give out my opinion. Well, I wish you could see Aily; you would see a second Milly, and if you saw the youngster you would have an exact third. My! how things change; it seems only yesterday since Milly was married, and since— but it's not good to be thinkin' too much. Now get over, Cagy, early. I will be on the lookout. Try and sleep. Let me fix the quilts about you. There; you're as comfortable as a bird in a nest. Good-night."

When his footsteps could be no longer heard, Cagy reached for his Bible. His candle was burning low, yet there was light enough to enable him to read the few lines that his eye had fastened on by accident:

"The days of man are short, and the

number of his months is with Thee: Thou hast appointed his bounds which cannot be passed."

A moth entangled itself in the sputtering light; the words were no longer legible. As he closed the book the candle went out. "Rob Roy" beneath him, marked with the one-eyed glass, now broken, was forgotten. The flickering glow of the dying pine log brought him strange thoughts and long-buried faces.

The morning came, one of great excitement for Squidville. If the truth were told, it would run that there were few sound sleepers in the village that night.

Daylight beheld a steady smoke from every chimney-pot, telling of expectations and bustle within. The Hunter's Paradise, a strange thing in its history, was kept open all night, and held little groups of villagers, amid smoke-puffs narrating all that was known of La Flamme, as well as venting a thousand conjectures as to his life in the far West. In this every man's imagination was free, and as a consequence there was no end of talk, so the night unnoticed had worn away, and the sun was feeling his way beyond the pines, scaling the mountains; the higher up he went the better was he to be seen. He was now tipping the chimneys, and throwing a kind of lantern-light on the roads.

That was enough to set life agog in a mountain town.

It was a saying that "a little light, with a bit of feeling, was enough for a mountaineer to guess his diggings."

Buttons' sleep was scant and jumpy. The first streak of light that blinked through the window-pane was a welcome excuse to jump from his bed and open his door to the morning's freshness.

He could hear the noise and note the lights in Weeks', an observation which on any other occasion would tickle his feet to tread in that direction. The present was little to his taste, bedded as he was in the past. He was nervous and sad. As he dressed the years slid past him, each a hideous spectre of vanished things. He had for the first time in his life fully awakened to the passing of things.

The thought rushed across his brain of the nothingness of Billy Buttons.

He went out into the keen air and whistled, giving music to his dancing brain-phantoms.

He looked towards the little graveyard, thought of La Flamme, and this somehow or other travelled his mind to Cagy. He but added a new figure.

When his wife called him to breakfast he was in a kind of dream, where he stood old and raggy by a grave marked Past. Strange, he was wishing to be there, not caring to march when all his love rested there.

As he sat at the table, his dream gone, he was moved to say audibly:

"There's not much in death, after all, when love is buried, and the future is a cold stranger. I rather think I'd like it."

This begot strange suspicions in the wife's head, who, womanly enough, remarked that "people ain't supposed to skip off because their friends do. I suppose you got those ideas from Cagy last night, who's sick a-cause of Frank's endin'."

"Cagy — ay, wife — Cagy — he should have been here, as he promised; he must be right sick in good earnest, so let one of the youngsters go and see if he can come."

The breakfast went on in silence until his stepson returned with the news that Cagy had a bad night. He was sorry that he could not get out, much less sit up in bed, and wanted pa to hurry over after the funeral. He would be a-thankin' Mrs. Buttons for a mug of gruel, very weak and a bit tasty, as his appetite was a kind of scratchy.

This news sorely depressed Buttons. He had an idea that when a man of Cagy's fibre came to a mug of gruel, and that having to be sweetened like a child's meal, the hunt was over.

With big tears jumping from wrinkle to wrinkle, he solemnly announced to his family that "Cagy would never draw a tricker, and as for me, to keep the gun long after he's gone is something that I don't expect." There was a family sob to punctuate this announcement.

Mrs. Buttons and family hastened to prepare the best they had in the most appetizing way for the sick man. Billy Buttons, sober and subdued, for the first time in his life keenly conscious of age, slowly sauntered to Weeks', there to await the little funeral cortège.

The coming was announced by the ringing of the church-bell. Up the village street came a country wagon containing a coffin, all that was mortal of La Flamme, drawn by two bay colts, followed by Squidville, "just," said a bystander, "a perfect image of the way his wife went to her long rest."

On went the cortège, the little bell "ringing its three rings, then takin' a bit of a breathin'-spell," until the cemetery was reached, and the brown-looking clay that told of a new grave approached. Standing there was Père Monnier, bent and broken on the wheel of time, looking in at the open grave with a sorrowful look, one that spoke of strange thoughts then tenanting his mind. Soon were grouped around him Aily, worn and sobbing, linking the past and present; her husband, giving rejected comfort; the child, full of wonder, not knowing whether to smile or cry; Weeks, holding its hand; Buttons, with the shovel that was to put his friend from mortal view.

The père spoke a few words of comfort, blessed Aily and her child, then tottered along the little path on his way to Cagy's.

"Ah, Billy!" said Weeks, lifting the child in his arms, "that's farewell to Frankie; and who'll be next? It looks as if the père is nearin' the end.

"Where is he going? My! how he totters; but he never complains. I said to him the other day that he should take a rest. What do you think he answers me? 'Jim, there will be a long rest some day, so as long as we can it is better to keep doing something.' That's him as long as I can remember—never himself, but his people. I'm not of his way of thinkin', but that never made the père a bit cooler to me and mine. Well, he's turning up by Cagy's, which makes me think that this gatherin' is a kind of queer without poor Cagy.

"I'll be a-gettin' that way myself. Come, Billy, we've crossed many a fence together."

"And I'm going," said the child. "Can't I go, ma, with Uncle Jim?"

"Better all go," was Aily's quiet reply. "Cagy, child, was grandma's uncle. He liked her as much as Uncle Jim likes you."

"And more, ay, more, Aily," muttered Weeks.

"He was also your grandpa's best friend and I was once his little girl. He kept that plot for my father, attended it, planted the flowers, and, being part of us in life, in death shall sleep among us."

"Is that the thing that killed grandpa? I don't like it!" cried the child.

They were at Cagy's house, amid his flowers and song-birds. The door was open, some one was reading; they stopped and listened. These words fell on their ears:

"He that loveth his neighbor hath fulfilled the law."

Then there was a pause, and they entered and gathered around the sick man's bed. Père Monnier closed the Bible and put it on the window-shelf, rose, whispered something in Cagy's ear, to which he replied:

"I'm ready, père; I'll go and look over the ground before you come. Farewell; everything is left for you to see to." The père then left.

"You're getting weaker, Cagy," said Buttons, "but rouse yourself; here's Aily, your little girl, come back; yes, Aily and another little Milly."

"Do, Cagy, sit up and see this child; she begs a kiss," said Weeks.

"Fix me up, Buttons; pillar me behind, a little sidewise. I want to get my good eye on you all. Poke over the child now; ay! that's a kiss that ought to make me better—if there was any betterin' to me. I have been in many a tough corner in my day, but this ends the hunt. Don't be blurting, Buttons; a man's days are numbered, and when the time comes let him hand in his gun with due reverence.

"I fixed up my account, temporal and spiritual, as best I knew; so I'm just awaitin' the call. I won't be lonely either; there's some one on the other side a-keepin' watch this many a day. I go off content, seein' you, Aily, and the certifier in your hand; besides this I want you to have my books. I stopped on 'Rob Roy,' page 243. Take that Bible, given by my mother; that's for little Milly. As to my home and belongings, that's Buttons'; all but my gun, that's for Jim.

"Everything is in tip-top shape, so I'm not complainin'.

"If you pull out the pillars, and let me down easy, I will be a bit better.

"Turn me over on my side; I want to have my one eye on the youngster."

"This is hard lines on me," said Buttons. "I don't see why I'm left, and Cagy gettin' ready to start."

"I pity poor Buttons," said Weeks; "it's long they've hunted together."

"Is there any hope?" said Aily, bending over her father's friend.

"Not much, I fear," said her husband; "he seems to be sinking since we put him down. See how strange his eyes are straining, as if he wished to see some one."

"He is smiling like a child," said Buttons,

holding his hand—"smiling as if he's happy. Listen; he's going to say something."

They listened; but one word fell from his lips—"Felina."

The spirit had fled.

On the little gravestone, a few weeks later, a man came and chiselled under Milly's name "Frankie: Cagy," and then La Flamme's dying wish:

"HOME AT LAST."

CHAPTER XI.

THE PASSING OF BILLY BUTTONS.

The making of the St. Lawrence & Adirondack Railway through Squidville was, perhaps, the biggest event in the history of that interesting town. It gave work to men, boys, horses, and, to apply a phrase that took life at that time, "everything was a-working, and what was not was eaten up." It was a truthful phrase, as most phrases coined by the common people are. Their language-coin is minted for use, and it is worth what it weighs. They do not slide around the bush, but aim right at the bull's-eye, a homely virtue in these days of mincing redundancies and delicate, bloodless word-phrasing. The farmer used his team, his boys were water-carriers, his beef was toothsome for the "bosses," his pork and potatoes the life of the workers. Spare oats and hay brought a good price. Chickens found a ready purchaser in the engineer corps. So everything was galloping in those times.

Towns are like individuals. A chance once comes to them of marring or making. The long-headed woodmen knew the difference. Mortgages were paid up; bits of land added to the original contract. Long-standing store-accounts, bequeathed from generation to generation, were cancelled. Men held their heads high, indulged in a couple of cigars a week, contracted buggies, and blanketed their horses.

It has been an observation of mine that in rural communities a man's wealth may easily be gauged by the look of the animals around his place. "Show me your company, and I will tell who you are," is an old saw. I suggest, Show me your barns, and I'll tell you what kind of a farmer you are. When barns are paintless, patchy, and rickety I look for a hole in the owner's hat, and a badly fitted patch, of a color other than the pants, on his knee-caps.

Long hair, squeaky boots, and pessimism may run in the same rut without astounding me. Man vibrates to environment. The music is dress.

Youngsters courted violently, the males donating largely such allurements as silver-tipped hair-combs, monogram rings, the metal of no consequence, the value lying in the extent to which it shone. Colored handkerchiefs, mostly silk, pocketbooks with a silver clasp, bracelets, candy artfully arranged that the package was a poetically composed love-letter. Candy played a prominent part that year. The bashful swain handed his love a "lozenger" with this blunt phrase, "Honey, will you be mine?" Gentle Phyllis checkmated him with this taking trump found in the same package, "Just name the day." Could there be anything so simple and yet so poetic as lay hidden in a package of Squidville candy? Billy Buttons, always ready to voice a fitting phrase, sold this candy as "Questions and Answers." These things being known, the wonderment ceases that marriages that year made bachelors so scarce as to be numbered on the two hands, not counting the thumbs.

And here I remark, for the benefit of the new woman, that in this lottery every man drew a prize, and treasured that prize more lovingly and ardently than on the lucky day he drew it. The reason, I think, is that the Squidvillite has learned that human nature will run easy when greased by love. That greasing he does not leave to his partner. He shoulders his share. What is heavy for one is light for two.

Married women bought shawls and new bonnets. They were not extravagant. They had economized on butter and eggs, until, unknown to their husbands, they had safely housed, in a newly knit stocking, the desired store of pennies. Then, some Sunday morning, the pennies were gone, but the shawl and hat were ready.

Children were kindly but forcibly reminded of the whipping that awaited them in case of disclosure of the secret to the father, who was just then enjoying, with the ease of a prince, a long projectile named "Rising Sun Cigar." When the bell rang its sweet invitation to come and worship God, and the husband called, "It's time for church, *ma cherie*, come 'veet,' " the wife, with a grave face, bonnet and shawl most artistically arranged, was soon by his side, carelessly looking into his eyes.

There was a quick heart-beat, a welling of love, a talking of eyes, and a kiss that set the children prattling. When the church-goers complimented him on the "youngness" of his wife he blushingly remarked:

"Ay, ay! It would be hard to find her equal. No mistake of that."

It was honorable pride, and a true setting of love.

As they homeward went laughingly he told her all the compliments paid her, and added his own, by far the most delightful to a good woman's ears. In them were the magic memories of life.

In the great business bustle Billy Buttons bore a distinguished part. The "lettering business" was increased one hundredfold, while the original bait of drawing customers by keeping a post-office showed itself a brilliant scheme. Trade was brisk. A man, while waiting for the assortment of his mail, saw many things to touch his pocketbook, and at reasonable prices.

The post-master's well-known honesty and perfect frankness in regard to his goods soon made his name known to the railway-camps. Then there were other attractions, dear to the tired workmen. Everybody was welcome to the post-office, and everybody free to tell his yarn, assured of a listening and approving crowd.

There was no flagging, as the master could always be depended on for a war- or hunting-story. To his credit be it written, the war-stories were not his own exploits. Hunting-stories gave him a wider range, and brought out more fully his great gifts as a born story-teller. In these, as hero, he divided honors with

Cagy, always giving due share to those wonderful dogs he had bred and trained.

Patronage such as this meant money, and by the time the railway was laid the post-master had, in various stockings and old shoes, the snug sum of two thousand dollars. A part of this was carried to his home; the remainder he kept in his office covered with old papers, mailed as a token of home love, but never called for by the owners.

It was, as he said, handy if one of his friends needed a "lift"; just in a place where he could get it easily, and no one was the wiser. His wife objected, the feminine element being noted in history as always suspicious of the future. Her ideas of thieves were foolish to his view. He called her reasonings "ravings," reminding her that his every cent was honestly got, and that no man or woman would steal from Billy Buttons. In her own way she was a logician, and argued that if thieves did not believe in honesty what did they care how honestly a thing was got if they could put their hands on it.

All this was adverse to the mind of her husband, and the old stockings and paper-stuffed shoe lay under the thousand weeklies, holding a bit of balm for the needy.

The post-master lived under a pretty delusion that no robber, no matter how acute he might be, would have brains enough "to poke amid old papers." Supported by this thought, he laughed at his wife's notions, and went on, day after day, augmenting the paper-heap.

Many a woman of Squidville, wanting papers to stuff holes and corners, came to him, knowing his large store, but with a laugh and a word he managed to baffle them and send them home in good humor.

"How can I give them," he would say, "as they ain't mine and I don't know when the owner might call? A post-master ain't like common folks; their papers are their own; mine belong to everybody. Besides, the papers I would give, perhaps, contain something better not known, so, all in all, I must do my duty and leave them where they are.

There was one man that knew of the treasure beneath the dusty, ill-kept heap, whose cat-eyes for a moment glimpsed at the stockings, and riveted themselves on the old shoe when its master took from it the full of his fingers of notes to help "a silly man that was trying to fool the people for a living, and, like a fool, was caught when he was making the biggest jump of his life."

When Corkey Slithers, bleeding and whining, was left with a warning to quit Squidville forever, Buttons returned home to harness his horse and start in quest of the fallen professor of occultism. He found him scarcely knowing what to do, and, arousing him to a sense of danger, he put him in his buggy and drove to the post-office.

Although it was the post-office talk for weeks that Corkey "was coining money, that he had struck a regular hail-storm in that line," Buttons was incredulous.

He had a poor idea of Squidville's individual generosity when it comes to pay for "capering that brings in nothing back."

To the Rev. Jamie Snooter, a travelling temperance-talker, who boasted of his conversions in all the mountain towns, and who boldly attacked Billy on smoking and drinking, clenching it down, as he said, with Billy's logic on capering, he replied, stamping the letters violently, "that smoking and drinking did give something back. Smoking soothed the mind and made his back memory flow like the Salmon River after a rain-

crop. A drink cured colic as fast as it struck it." The audience, mostly a crowd of experimentalists, were with Buttons, and openly laughed at what they called "the snooterings of Mr. Snooter."

When Weeks heard of Billy's brilliant dash against Snooter he could not eat his dinner until he had congratulated him. "Just a bit of rock-sense I put against the Rev. Jamie's froth, making his arguments more suddy than when they struck me. Folks that have a bit of learnin' nowadays," continued he, "will have a hobby—not for saving man, but making themselves a bit known. The country is full of sham and shoddy, Jim Weeks."

The quiet laugh and the slow head-shake of the hotel-man were convincing of his sympathies on this point.

Corkey, when asked pointblank if "by his capering he had made any money," whiningly denied, confirming Buttons in his suspicions.

"I trusted," he said, and, seeing now that his art was ruined by an unholy contact with science, he had no hopes of collecting. "People will say 'fraud,' not knowing how the spirit, observing, as only a spirit can, the use of the doctor's syringe, concealed in his big pocket, vanished at the moment of action, throwing me in full shot of the doctor's fluid and tangling me with a perplexing gown. The common mind is unable to reason out such obscurities, and hence, Mr. Post-master, it avails itself of that destructive word *fraud*. Call a sane dog mad, and he will be clubbed to death. Say fraud, and woe to the victim.

"May I trust that I am particularly understood, William Buttons?"

"Hush your clattering, Corkey. Your learnin' and speechifying has been your blight. I fear your mainspring is out of kelter. I wish I had a looking-glass till you would see what a spectacle you've come to. Your face has cracks on it that soap won't thaw out. You were never much noted for beauty, with all your puttying and powdering and sweet-water sprinkling, but now no concoction could make you passable in a crowd. Poor Corkey, you are like an effigy of something a fellow might think he would meet in the woods. Faith, the preacher had a head on him when he said, 'Put it in your skulls and keep it there; observin' will confirm it. Beauty's skin deep; no more, no less.'

"The observin' is all on you, Corkey. The

only woman you can court now is a blind one; even her, if she has good feelin', will note the ruts. But, Corkey, misfortune should learn you a bit," and Buttons on one knee fumbled amid the papers, exposing stockings and diving into the old shoe, bringing out the full of his fingers of notes and closing Corkey's hand upon them. The papers were carelessly kicked until the treasure was again hidden. "Take this, Corkey. It's all for the days when you were courting Milly La Flamme; all for those days. There was no tucks then in your skull; you were an honest man, and doing fine work, training the young.

"I don't forget how you set the Poulets reading and spelling until they could cipher out anything in print. Many a time, too, you gave me a lift in the lettering. So, for all you done in those old days, take the bills, Mr. Corkey. Go somewhere and follow out your profession, and leave your spirit business to bigger fools. Come, let us be getting out of Squidville if you fear a tattered hide."

Corkey, casting a wistful look at the old papers, was soon in the buggy, waving his hand and saying: "Farewell to Squidville! And while I take issue with you, Billy Buttons, whether I shall lie in roses, or, as now, stumble amid briars and thorns, your name shall scintillate passionately through memory's cells, every vibration telling of your goodness."

"The moon is just right for bears," remarked Buttons as he took his seat beside Slithers. "I'll bet they'll be nibbling corn to-night. Many such nights Cagy and I were afoot under her glance. She filled my mind with thinkin'. When she's shining, just as she is now, that, says I, is Buttons when all is going his way. When she dips under a cloud, that, too, says I, is Buttons in hard luck. Corkey, you should think of these things. You're down, but you will, if you take care of yourself, be some day on the ups."

His moralizing was rudely broken by Slithers, who rather sang than spoke:

"Farewell, a long farewell to the pleasant banks of the Salmon, whose soft music gurgles in the ears of your fervent admirer, Corkey Slithers."

"A funny world this," thought Buttons. "Gee up!" and the knowing horse assumed his gait.

They drove to the little coal-box station to catch the early train for Montreal.

Squidville awoke next morning, and, in fury, rushed to the professor's den. But the bird had flown.

A few of the ardent spirits started to seek the "swindler" by the various roads that led from Squidville. On one of these they met William Buttons coming at an easy jog, pipe in hand singing:

> "Je tiens cette maxime utile
> De ce fumeux monsieur de Crac.
> En champagne comme à la ville
> J'adore l'amour et le tabac.
>
> "Quand ce grand homme allait en guerre
> Il portrait, dans son petit sac :
> Le don portrait de sa bergere,
> Avec la pipe de tabac."

As they came within hailing distance he was greeted with: "Buttons, we're looking for Corkey, and we'll end him. Have you seen him? Were you on the hunt?"

Putting his two hands to his mouth, in the shape of a boat, the better to convey sound, he informed the hunters, much to their disgust, that there was no use in following up the trail, as it would be lost at the station. "He's gone, and forever." There was a halt and a turning of buggies. Corkey had safely fled.

Banks were made for the thrifty and careful. Their existence was not unknown to Buttons, who, in earlier years, had made a deposit of twenty-five dollars, but drew it out the same day, to the disgust and with the grumbling of the cashier, to help to bury the wife "of a poor cuss" whose ills constant never took him prepared.

The cashier's anger, opening in a curse, left in Buttons' mouth an unwholesome taste of all money-houses. He was wont to say, and I am far from taking the negative, that "civility in such institutions is a polish that thickens or lessens according to the rank of the depositor." I often wondered if it was not on account of this polish that bank-clerks were so much sought after to take classes in Sunday-schools. If they were not so migratory, and so uncertain oftentimes of returning, in this occupation their success had been long ago proverbial. As it is, thanks to the polish so necessary to institutions where crafty civility is a law of life, they are always preferred to the workingman. Despite the twaddle we hear and read of the dignity of labor, the dignity of dress is higher. The moralists fume about the hidden diseases, of the rottenness within, of the whiteness without, but talk is merely a matter of their craft. When the rottenness is hidden by a few yards of silk, or even costly broadcloth, these same moralists are mesmerized, and either deny the disease or call it by some name that takes away the odium. Unsavory smells may, for the time, appear sweet with a liberal quantity of perfumery.

Buttons cared little for surface-polish—that not-to-be-despised vesture which so often has masked depravity for years.

He despised, by his conduct, the dictum of the cynical Talleyrand, who declared that speech was made to hide thought. Buttons was not civilized enough for such a dictum; he was not sufficiently emasculated. A spade was a spade, and he thought it was right to call it such in company. Think of this mountaineer defining it as "an instrument by which clay may be turned over"! Words were to him for the expression of what he felt. They were clean-cut, and went to the bull's-eye at once. His booklearning was scanty, but ably seconded by common-sense—a lack that gives to modern booklore a hieroglyphic appearance. Yet may not the reader, thinking of the pile of waste paper and its hidden treasure, thank Heaven that their common-sense is of another kind—a kind

♠

that would save them from such carelessness. Their common-sense would lead them to a bank, where polish would greet them, and civility, bowing, would take their money. Buttons might lose his money by a thief; once the hiding-place was known the taking were easy. The depositor might lose his, as he has often done.

What difference, then, there must be between polish and a common thief! The one is a thief; the other an absconder, a bank-wrecker. There is no difference, you exclaim; it is a playing of words—mere cant. Be it so, for it is so; and the sooner you learn that cant is our ordinary coin, and either learn it and be worldly, or abhor it and withdraw into your cave, the wiser will men deem you. Would you reform all this—an Augean stable? If you would, call not your task a reformation. That word has lost its original meaning, although grave Dr. Trench has taken no notice. An elevation of one's self, by any and every means, at somebody's expense, will be its definition by the future lexicographer.

Buttons was too near nature to have polish, and his life was spent among those who had not studied the dictum of M. Talleyrand.

These are the only valid reasons I may give: Lack of polish and cant, which made Buttons leave, year after year, his hard-earned store in an old shoe, a poor safe, its door but a stuffing of old paper, when he might have had it in security and at interest.

Custom has a parasitic growth. The passing years, and the old shoe's safety, were convincing that security can lie in a bundle of newspapers. To this thought he accustomed himself, and rarely, unless when needful, bothered himself about the money.

Age had come upon him not gently, he held, but "with a cat-spring." He was peevish under her meshes. His had been a life in the open—a communing with Nature in all the forms she presents in the Adirondacks. These forms were many, and to her lover ever delightful. In spring, the dark green stretches of cedar and pine, sentinelling the cool, child-laughing Salmon. The speckled beauties mischievously lurking under the sun-dried rock, in their eagerness for prey biting at an illusion as he warily drew the fly in their way. Then the thrilling hiss of the line, and the merry music of the reel, and the sunlight on the delicate colors, as, pluckily fighting, their owner ran alongside the boat to death and the fisherman's basket. In summer, the lone boating on the loveliest of lakes, robins spilling music along his route— a nosegay at every landing. In autumn, the glorious deer-hunt and ravishing dog-music. All is quiet; then a sharp bark. Your eyes are strained in the direction of the dog, and your gun unconsciously follows the motion of the eye. There is a lull; the music has stopped; disgust sits on your face, and the gun hangs stupidly by your side. Faith is pinned to the dog. The crafty, cunning fellow deserves your faith. Through briars and thorns and ragged choke-cherries, not caring a button for a blood-speck on his hide, he has followed his prey, circled with him in the spruce, followed him to the edge of the pine, dogged him by the mountain brooks, across the glade, over the mountains, backwards and forwards, keeping your spirits dancing to the mad, merry music of his tongue. And nearer and nearer the music comes! quicker, sharper, surer, a ring of triumph in it, trembling by times, always exulting. The gun is ready—it no longer hangs by the side; the hold is one steady for action—the eyes are quick and jerky. Nor is there long to wait. With the softness of an evening breeze the majestic fellow — Apollo, with the sandals of Hermes—divides the brush, his antlers thrown back, his perfect nose testing danger, his ears quick, decisive, catching every sound, his big black eyes pools of pity.

The dog knows not mercy, and his wild music has brought the brute within to the surface. The brute has no ideas of beauty, and to him pity is unknown. The dog taunts you—he has done his duty. Comrades are listening for the welcome shot, which shall conjure up visions of venison, and a good story for the camp-fire. A crack, quick, airy, goes booming through the woods, strays around the edges of the lakes, and dies. It is enough. Comrades rejoice. A jump, a piercing bleat, like a sheep when on a stormy night she has lost her young, a throwing forth of the majestic head, a snappy twitch of the body — the hunt is over — the deer is dead. Closer comes the dog in sight of his prey, proud of his master's prowess, wildly leaping, shaking his head, wagging his tail, lying beside the fallen monarch, lapping his blood, the petted and spoiled, reading in his master's eye the only trophy that is worth trying for—love.

Keen as was Buttons' vim for sport, Cagy tells where it was paralyzed by the spell of beauty.

Those who believe that beauty is a quality only sought after by the cultured (and it is an opinion violently held) live in their own domain. The poor man's wife, who in the burning, sapping city, rears a consumptive geranium in some old canister, wearily awaiting the blasted bud to flower, worships beauty. The poor man's child, in her first country walk, who rolls in the green grass so soft, from her raggy carpet, and kisses the buttercups, or who chases the mottled butterfly and fixes her curls, the brook her mirror, the comb her fingers, is a lover of beauty. Love is universal, and wherever the watchful imp goes his mantle is beauty.

The story runs that one day Billy Buttons, tired of hearing dogs, and seeing no game, lay down on a green patch by the Salmon River, a patch hid by a few stunted willows, and went into deep slumber for a few hours. He awoke carefully, as was his fashion, to find a few rods from him a huge buck, throwing cooling showers over his back and refreshing himself for a new run. The sight was so beautiful that—I quote William's language: "I could not draw a tricker to save my life. I scared the fellow away, and when the dogs came up and crossed the stream I leashed them. Everything should have one chance, while they're living, for their life."

To these delights of autumn add that of the forest shading itself into winter; see the green clasping yellow; the yellow drifting into wine-color, then darker and darker, until it reaches the dark brown gnarled leaf nipped by a baby frost, the idle sport of every scampering gale. What is more palatable to the artistic in man than the silvery thread of the river stoled in green just as the sun lies down to rest, breathing twilight with his last beams, draining his last goblet to the moon's short and mystic reign?

How often had Buttons gazed on such scenes brewing sadness, his soul not deigning to give its thoughts speech-setting.

Nor was winter less full of pleasantry to this lover of nature. The jingle of sleigh-bells, the mountain dances, the dashing hunts after the fox, the retelling of folk-lore by the crackling pine-wood—these made a joyous time, and winter was as welcome as her lighter-dressed sisters.

Age had come. I had written to Billy Buttons, and times had changed. Old faces had slipped away; new ones wore a strange air. The rude mountain town was changing into a conventional country village. Parties were springing up, and selfishness growing. The strangers, who knew him not, tried to have the post-office in new hands, and, this failing, weekly petitioned Washington for a business post-master. Yes, that horrid word "business" was prefixing itself to everything and everybody, and dealing death-blow to the pleasant life of early Squidville.

The friends of his youth had gone. Some, like Père Monnier and Cagy, were sleeping their last sweet sleep; others, like Weeks, had sold out and gone West to join the Mintons. Billy Buttons no longer visited the Hunter's Paradise, whose name had been changed to the Brunswick. The new owner was spruce and spry. He had enlarged the premises, painted them a gaudy color, businesslike. Your ordinary tourist loves show. There was a large card in the office, limiting the privileges of guides. Buttons being post-master, these privileges might have been extended; but he was not the man to sail under false colors. "Guiding is my life-work," he warmly said. "This lettering affair was something the boys put upon me, so I keep it for their sake, and if they were around to-day there would be no sneaking after it. It's easy seen my partners got the start of me in the long journey."

Nor was the little church the same. The new minister had neither the devotion nor the winning ways of Père Monnier. He loudly voiced the complaint against the post-master's way of doing business. He rarely called on him, and, when he did, his signs of being bored at the old hunter's tales were evident.

"Perhaps it is," said Buttons, "because I am always telling him of Père Monnier. I am sorry it vexes him, but a man *must* speak of his own life; and the best part of mine was Père Monnier. These woods shall never see his like again. Just the kind of a man that Christ, as I know Him, would have said to 'come and follow Me,' and made him an apostle right on the spot. Well, he's gone ahead, and although I'm rough material from him, I ain't a bit afraid to follow. As he used to say, 'God won't expect much from them that haven't overmuch to bank on, and if you follow me I'll show you the way,' and I may have been a little roundabout, but I never got lost that I couldn't find the trail, and if I brought a little mud with me it was washed away. If the wise man fell seven times a day, repented, and came to grace, do you have grit. There's aye a chance for you, Buttons. And when I do get in beside Cagy and Frank and his wife—I don't care how high they are that Père Monnier's with, he'll come down and take my hand. I remember him one day talking to a big man. There was a crowd around him when I and Cagy, in our worst clothes, passed. He broke away from the rich folk and called to us, 'Boys, is it passing your pastor you are and not giving him a *bon jour?* It's the least you could do.'

" 'Seeing you were engaged,' says I, 'and us in our working-rags—'

" 'Nonsense!' says he; 'nonsense! You're my own people, and clothes makes no man.' Thumping us on the heart, 'If that's clean, you're gentlemen.' And a cigar went to each of us.

" 'Buttons,' says Cagy, 'will you ever forget this day? It's as sacred to me as my Bible. May the Lord spare him his health many a day, to thump men's hearts and drive in his little bit of balm.'"

Buttons was not resentful to these changing things. He spoke of them more with sadness than bitterness. He reckoned that his days were numbered, and he hoped that when his hour came he would, with courage and decency, pass over to his fathers. There was one longing, for life has its hobbies to the end. That longing was to die as post-master of Squidville-town.

His homely phrase was, to die in harness. Age has its hobbies as well as youth, and clings more tenaciously to them. The death of a hobby is a chip from the block of life. It was useless to argue old age,—that is uncomplimentary and in bad taste,—physical debilities, which meant memories of health, a contrast fraught with sadness, for giving up the post-office. He was heedless, firm in resolve to die in the lettering business. The grocery trade had been gladly turned over to his stepsons, the Poulets, with the distinct understanding that the corner sacred to letters was sacred to Buttons.

I think he was right. Possibly he came to his idea by sound logic. Logic does exist outside the schools. In other days, when spry and joyous, I had heard him say:

"If you want to kill an old man quick let him have nothing to do."

To that same idea I adhere—experience in my case makes it a truth.

Old age is prone to ask questions from the future, and to no age will that mysterious nymph unveil. To be thus thwarted, I grant, is not pleasant. Then comes lone-voiced sadness, and the best cure is work. Continually to live in the future is to ignore the present, and to be untaught of the past. "Live well to-day and you will make the best preparation for the morrow," was a practical text of Père Monnier. Buttons kept his little corner fenced in with stout railing as his own preserve.

He had become a great reader, and he had the country post-master's well-known and respected right of reading all the newspapers that came to his office. It was not unfrequent to hear the farmer ask, "Billy, had you time to give it a glance?" referring to his weekly newspaper. These glimpses kept the old post-master busy when not receiving and distributing mail.

Day by day he hobbled to and fro between his house and his office attended by an aged hound, the master's gait seeming to suit the dog's. This hound was dear to the old man's heart. It was a dying present of Père Monnier to the post-master. The père loved a dog and gun—things that endeared him to early Squidville.

It was meet that his champion dog, Mickey Free, whose wonderful skill in deer-tracking had won the heart of the guides for his master, should be left, when that master was no more, to the watchful tendance of loving hands, in other words, to William Buttons. An old dog, his master dead, kept for show, not for love, is a sad sight. In Buttons' case there was a double love—love for the man of men, love for the intrinsic worth of Mickey, whose cunning had given Buttons many a shot.

So they toddled together. When Sunday came the dog left him at the church door hunting every nook of the garden for his old master.

No inducement could make him enter the parsonage or make friends with the new rector. His faithfulness and lonesomeness welled up many a memory in the parishioners' hearts. When the service was over he took his place by his master's side.

"There goes the père's dog and Billy Buttons," said the parishioners.

Winter had come, more than unusually cold and stormy. Roads were bad, walking puzzling, even to the young. Buttons would not be home-bound, so there was only one way, said his family, to settle matters. A bed came to the office, and an old sleeveless coat as a shake-down for Mickey. The Poulets would see that their father wanted nothing. This move captivated Billy Buttons.

"Don't bother yourself," he said, "carting me any food. The store's full of all kinds of canned goods, fit enough for Bonaparte and his officers. I'll be like the rats—nibble here and there when you're not around. Me and Mickey will get along, never fear. If we can't do anything else, we can sit and look out of the window and watch the woods and think. I guess he's like myself. If he hunts any more it will be with his memory."

This life was to his taste, and his taste was respected. Billy Buttons and Mickey Free, man and dog bound together by mutual ties of love, took up their winter quarters in the post-office.

The post-master was an early riser. Long years of practice had confirmed him in his habit. The first puff of smoke in the village came from his chimney. It kept many a clock in order.

"Set her about five minutes past five. Buttons smokes, and you'll be close to the right," was a common expression.

The stepsons came a few hours later.

One morning there was no smoke from Buttons' chimney. This troublesome fact was noticed by Mrs. Buttons. She had, as often before, strange dreams through the night. She dreamt she saw Cagy prepare a bed of roses, and when she asked him what he was doing that for he smiled and said "that it was a bed for one who lived up to his lights."

Being further impelled by human curiosity to inquire who was the lucky one, Cagy breathed her husband's name, and went out of her sight like a hawk when she was looking at him. Then she awoke. Mickey was savagely barking, but as he had often done that before it gave her but little thought. Now she had something to spin, three strands of yarn to twist into a tale. Nervous by nature, suspense became anguish. Her sons were aroused and her fears made known. They argued that their father might have been sick, thus allaying the smoke theory; the dog's barking betokened little, but when they came to the dream, they met it with laughter.

Laughter makes no converts. It may effect a prudent silence, and silence so glibly prated as consent is a falsity which passes with unleavened minds for truth. Truth-tasting as an occupation employs but few. Mrs. Buttons would be convinced when her sons would return. As they made ready to comply with her wishes, a neighbor in a hurry for his breakfast came with the news that he went to the office for groceries necessary for that meal, and "knocked—knocked for fully a good ten minutes, and neither Billy nor the dog let on, which was a bit queer, so I came to get one of the boys to open and let me have what I want, as it's getting well on."

Mrs. Buttons' suspicions were being confirmed. Her spinning was not in vain. The boys and neighbor hurried ahead. Youth runs well. Age and Mrs. Buttons came trotting after. Her mind was full of rude thinking, a land of dark and depressing shadows. An old shawl was carelessly twisted around her small, drooping form, the wind flapping its ends.

"Mother," cried the boys, "go back to the house, put something on your head, and take off your slippers. You'll surely be laid up after this. It will be a nice mess, you and father sick together." The language was rough as a cocoanut-shell, but it had milk of kindness within.

She heeded them not, impelled by her mind-spinning. The cold was keen and bitingly blown by the wind, yet she felt it not. When the mind is mad the body is forgotten.

On she went, hoping, doubting, reaching the post-office door as her sons were preparing to burst it open.

"Wait!" she cried. "Knock louder. Let me call him. If he is not dead entirely, when he hears my voice he will answer."

They obeyed her wish. They pounded the door first with their strong fists, then with stones, letting her raise her weak voice to its highest pitch. No answer came to change her anguish. Tears clothed her eyes, a piercing sob came to her lips.

"Break in the door," said the neighbor, "he may be only unconscious. You know, Mrs. Buttons, he was an old man, and the old oftentimes get fainting-fits. A little water will recruit him. Just duck it over his face and rub him up good. I'll run and get some." He went.

Where there is a will there is a way, and there were both will and way in breaking the door of the post-office. As it fell inside Mrs. Buttons entered, treading her way on it calling:

"Billy, it's me—your wife. Where are you?"

Grief had blinded her. There he lay, a few feet from her, bleeding, dead. At the shoulder of his extended right arm lay the nose of Mickey, his form hardly recognizable. The bloody floor-track told that, dying, he had crawled up to his dead master and, resting on the arm that had so long fondled him, breathed his last.

"My dream! my dream!" said the widow. "Sure enough he's with Cagy to-day, and if dogs could go poor Mickey would follow his master."

She knelt by her husband's side in his blood, muttering a hasty prayer. Then, passion conquering grief, she raised her eyes and clasped hands, asking vengeance of God. Sorrow, henceforth, was to gangrene her life. Some day death would come as a respite.

The store showed evidence of a violent struggle, in which the dog bore no insignificant part. A back window, shattered to pieces, was convincing proof that by this way the murderer had gained admittance. His coming aroused the dog, who in turn would awake his master. As Buttons lay in his nightgown in the middle of the store, it was evident that he was aware of the intruder's design, and hastened to give him battle. The bullet-holes told of unequal strife. Yet, the bloody iron bar, lying as it fell from the dead man's hands, and the crimson stains leading from the broken window through the brush, lost in the slightly frozen river, were convincing that the slayer would carry through life scars of the old woodsman's defence.

The winter had passed—a winter full of work. Thousands of logs had been drawn to the Salmon River, ready for the thaw and the first freshlets to start them down to Dixon's saw-mill. Spring came with her nimble and delicate fingers, plucking leaves from buds, with her wand changing the breaking, grumbling ice into crystal pools, throwing bits of green here and there to light up the cold fields and mock the hilltop patches of snow.

How the logs shot, jumped, dived, playing like river-snakes in the slobbery waters, the sun shining on their moss-covered backs! The river's bank had a merry crew to watch their antics and keep them in order. This land-coming fellow was shoved to the current; that "lagger" made, with a well-directed prod of the "cant-hook," to quicken his pace.

A few of the logs, caught by an eddy, were whirled into the mouth of a brook. As the driver dislodged them his hook brought with it a man's body.

When it lay on the shore, surrounded by the

drivers, a suggestion of the "boss" was followed by one of his men "to search the corpse's pockets for means of identification."

Stuffed in the inside pocket was an old shoe full of bills, some of them fringed with blood. Each of the trouser-pockets held a stocking half-filled with gold.

"That's all," said the searcher. "His money didn't do him much good. I wonder if there's anything for us in this find. If I had a little of the yellow stuff I think I could warm you on it. You'll find the coroner won't let this pile go through his hands, as big as it is; no, it's too sticky."

"You didn't try his inside vest-pocket," said the boss. "Often folks keep their letters there; it won't do any harm to try. One of you count the money in the shoe, for fear that there be any trouble hereafter."

"To begin with," said the driver who began the count, "here is a check. I wish you would cipher it out." "Here's two old envelopes," said the pocket-searcher, "for you after you get through; there's some kind of scrawling on them."

"This is a check," said the boss, "payable to William Buttons, and made out to the same by

Narcisse Monnier. I think that's the reading. The wet has blurred it a little."

"That's it," said one of the crowd. "Billy told me that he had one of them for five dollars, but as it was the only bit of writin' he had of the père, he wouldn't change it for no money."

"You're right. It's for a five," said the boss.

"The envelope is plain enough:

Mr. Corkey Slithers, T. O. S.,

whatever that means."

"Throw the villain into the river; smash him among the logs! We know who killed Buttons now," were the savage cries of the excited group.

"Be calm, calm, boys," said the boss. "He's dead; you can't injure him. 'Vengeance is Mine, saith the Lord.'"

www.ingramcontent.com/pod-product-compliance
Lightning Source LLC
Chambersburg PA
CBHW031952230426
43672CB00010B/2140